MODERN PROBLEMS IN THE ANCIENT WORLD

FRANK BURR MARSH, PH.D.
Late Professor of Ancient History
The University of Texas

The University of Texas Press
AUSTIN: 1943

CONTENTS

INTRODUCTION

PART ONE ATHENS

Chapter I. Solon and the "New Deal" in Athens

Chapter II. Unemployment and Imperalism

PART TWO ROME

Chapter I. Agricultural Depression and the Army

Chapter II. Machine Politics and Efficiency

Chapter III. The Breakdown of Constitutional Government

NOTE ABOUT THE AUTHOR

The gifted author of these essays was an international authority on the early Roman Empire. His first book in the field, *The Founding of the Roman Empire*, was published by The University of Texas in 1922. In 1927, Oxford University Press republished this volume in a revised edition, and followed it in 1931 with *The Reign of Tiberius*, in which Professor Marsh presented a searching analysis of Tacitus and to a considerable degree exonerated Tiberius of the charges and implications of his classical critic. In 1935 Methuen and Company published his *History of the Roman World, 146 to 30 B.C.*, and this was reissued in an American edition by the Macmillan Company in 1939. In the meantime, he published a dozen or more penetrating articles between 1925 and 1932 in *The American Historical Review, Classical Journal, Classical Quarterly*, and *Classical Philology*. An earlier book, *English Rule in Gascony, 1199–1252*, was published at Ann Arbor in 1912.

Professor Marsh was born in Michigan, March 4, 1880, and died in Dallas, Texas, May 31, 1940. He was graduated from the University of Michigan with the degrees of A.B. and Ph.D., studied at the University of Paris, was instructor in history at the University of Michigan for several years, and came to The University of Texas as instructor in history in 1910. The three chapters on Roman history, comprising Part II of this little volume, were delivered in the form of lectures while Professor Marsh was holding the honorary appointment of Research Professor in the Graduate School of The University of Texas during 1934. The parallel which they inevitably disclosed between Rome during the first century B.C. and the United States two thousand years later was so striking that there was an immediate demand for publication. In preparation for such publication, Professor Marsh wrote the two

chapters on Athenian developments, comprising Part I of this
book; but for one reason or another publication continued to be
delayed.

This posthumous appearance of the author's last serious work
seems a fitting memorial to his industry, his lovable personality,
and his critical scholarship, which lent much credit to the
Graduate School of The University of Texas. The manuscript
has been carefully read by Professor Marsh's good friend and
colleague, Dr. Harry J. Leon, Professor of Classical Languages,
who has made slight revisions. To those who knew Professor
Marsh, it is unnecessary, but to others it may be desirable,
to say that his study was wholly without social or political
purport. It was always his concern to present an objective
picture of his findings and leave his readers to draw their own
conclusions—not that he had no convictions—and it is in his
spirit that these essays are published.

The book was designed by Mr. C. C. Kinney of The University of Texas Department of Art. It was published under
a grant from The University of Texas Research Institute.

EUGENE C. BARKER.

The University of Texas,
December 15, 1942

NOTE BY THE AUTHOR

The three chapters on Rome are based on the lectures which I delivered as the Research Professor of The University of Texas for 1933–34. I wish to take this opportunity to thank my colleague, Professor P. M. Batchelder, for many helpful suggestions in preparing these studies for publication.

F. B. M.

Austin, Texas.
Jan. 1, 1937.

INTRODUCTION

There is an old saying that history repeats itself, and, like most such sayings, this one is both true and false. From the earliest times men have been confronted by the same fundamental problems and have sought to solve them in much the same ways. In a sense, therefore, history has continually repeated itself from the beginning. The repetition, however, has never been exact. The fundamental problems may have been the same, but they have never presented themselves twice under exactly the same conditions. Unemployment on a scale such that something had to be done about it is nothing new in human experience, and the number of remedies which *could* be contrived is so limited that the same methods of dealing with the problem have been tried over and over again. Yet the circumstances under which the problem arose and under which the solution of it was attempted have never precisely duplicated themselves. While, therefore, history has many valuable lessons to teach, they are not to be learned by a rapid glance at the outward course of events. We cannot hastily conclude that because a certain remedy failed to solve some problem in the past it will necessarily fail in the present. We must first determine precisely *why* the remedy failed in the past and then examine present conditions to see whether the causes of failure are still at work, whether they are as potent as they once were, and whether any new factors exist which may affect the result. It is only by serious and careful study that history can be made to serve as a useful guide to human conduct.

These considerations are perhaps somewhat trite and obvious, but they have an application to the present work. The author has no expectation that the brief studies that follow will throw any new light on the problems which confront the world today. In another way, however, he hopes that they may be found to have some interest and value. It is his belief that the ancient Greeks and Romans were forced to meet some of the same problems which we are now trying to solve, and that, if we examine certain phases of ancient history in the light of our recent experience, we shall find ourselves viewing them in a somewhat new perspective and with a somewhat better understanding. If this should prove to be true in even a small degree, the purpose of the present work will have been achieved.

Among the modern problems which were prominent in ancient times three stand out rather obviously, namely, agricultural depression, unemployment, and the breakdown of constitutional government. The purpose of the studies which follow is to show how these problems arose in Athens and in Italy and how the Athenians and the Romans solved or failed to solve them.

PART I

ATHENS

I

SOLON AND THE "NEW DEAL" IN ATHENS

In the seventh century B.C. there was a prolonged depression in Athens, and the distress of the common people became so great that finally Solon was elected archon with extraordinary powers in the hope that he, a man who commanded the respect and confidence of all parties, would be able to find some remedy for the existing discontent, which was reaching the point where a violent explosion seemed probable. His reforms marked an epoch in Athenian history and have naturally been much discussed by modern historians. Perhaps it is superfluous to add that the discussion has not resulted in complete agreement. Our information in regard to him and his work is derived chiefly from two sources, a biography by Plutarch and Aristotle's treatise on the Athenian constitution. Not only are both these accounts very brief, but on some points they contradict each other. The first step, therefore, is to decide which of the two is the more trustworthy. Here there can be little doubt that the preference should be given to Aristotle, but Plutarch's biography was known to scholars long before the treatise on the Athenian constitution, which was only recovered toward the close of the nineteenth century. The traditional view of Solon, therefore, was based solely on Plutarch, and it has maintained itself to a considerable degree in spite of the new evidence so recently come to light. Fortunately both Plutarch and Aristotle quoted somewhat freely from certain poems which Solon wrote to explain and justify his work to his contemporaries, so that on some points we have the testimony of the reformer himself. Nevertheless, it is impossible to clear away all doubts and uncertainties, but most of these are of little importance for our present purpose.

In Athens, when Solon became archon, the economic condition of a large part of the common people was desperate. Although many details are uncertain, the most striking feature in the situation was debt slavery. This institution is a common one and is found in all parts of the world among peoples at a certain stage of civilization. If a debtor was unable to pay, his property was seized, and if that was insufficient, he and his family could be sold as slaves. Now in Attica there were a comparatively few large estates and many small farms. The small farmer found himself obliged to borrow from his richer neighbor and when, as very frequently happened, he could not pay, he lost first his land and then his freedom. This process had been going on for a long time and the consequences were what we might naturally expect. As the poor got poorer and the rich richer, discontent became general and the danger of a revolution became constantly greater. The basic causes of the depression cannot be determined with certainty, but according to the best guess we can make there were two. In the first place, many of the farms were too small to support their owners, and in the second, the raising of grain, which was apparently the main crop, may have been becoming less profitable, for the Greeks had begun to import wheat from the Black Sea region and it seems likely that the small farmer in Attica would find it difficult to compete with the imported grain. This explanation must remain conjectural, for our information on the point is very scanty.

At any rate, from whatever cause, agricultural distress seems to have steadily increased in Attica, and about 630 B.C. a man named Cylon sought to take advantage of the prevailing unrest to set himself up as what the Greeks called a tyrant and what we should call a dictator. His attempt was defeated, but even the rich saw that something must be done, or another attempt would be made by someone else, perhaps with better success. In 621 B.C., therefore, Draco was given authority to reduce the law to writing, and, if Aristotle is correct, to reform the constitution. His work, however, brought little alleviation of the situation and discontent continued to grow. Not only was the danger of a tyrant still present, but a "share the wealth," that is to say "redivide the land," program found numerous adherents. At length matters became so critical that Solon was called on to save society. He was himself a man of wealth, but he had never taken sides with any of the parties of the day. He was generally believed to be honest and impartial, and everyone seems to have hoped that he would be able to find some way to better the existing conditions. He assumed the office of Archon with extraordinary powers in 594 B.C. and at once proceeded to attack the depression with a "new deal." Many of the details of this "new deal" are very obscure, but some of its main features are clear enough, since in regard to them we have the testimony of Solon himself.

His first step was to cancel all mortgages on land and to free all those who had been reduced to slavery on account of debt, permitting those who had fled from Athens to escape such a fate to return. He also managed to secure the freedom of many debt slaves who had been sold abroad, although how he accomplished this we are not informed. In addition to these measures he enacted a law forbidding debt slavery for the future. Whether the cancellation of debts applied to anything except mortgages on land it is impossible to say with certainty. Both Aristotle and Plutarch speak simply of a cancellation of debts, from which we should infer that all debts

were cancelled, but Solon in the passages quoted from his
poems speaks only of mortgages. Perhaps he allowed other
debts to stand and contented himself with prohibiting the
seizure of the debtor's person in case he was unable to pay.
This would seem the more likely from a story told of Solon.
While he was considering his debt legislation, he discussed the
matter with some of his most intimate friends. Learning his
intentions in advance, they hastened to borrow money on their
land and with it to purchase more. When Solon issued his
decree cancelling all mortgages, they had their old land free
and clear and the new land as well. We are told that this
brought much suspicion on Solon, which was dissipated by his
remitting a number of debts which were owed to him. Plutarch
adds that he did this in accordance with his law, but this
seems rather absurd, since he could hardly make an exception
in his own case. If all debts, however, were not cancelled by
his decree then one can see very well how he could meet
criticism by remitting debts which the law did not touch.
Probably to most of the poorer class who were not landowners
the prohibition of debt slavery was the same thing as the cancellation of their debts, but there must have been some merchants and craftsmen to whom it made a very appreciable difference, since they had some property to lose and many of
them, perhaps, could pay if they tried.

Perhaps to help the debtors whom his cancellation of mortgages had not affected, Solon devalued the drachma by a little
less than a third. It is possible, however, that this measure was
prompted by other motives. There were at this time in the
Greek world two standards of currency, one of which prevailed
on the mainland and the other among the islands of the Aegean.
Athens had hitherto followed the continental standard, but her
commercial relations were bound to be principally with states

using the other, and Solon may have aimed at facilitating exchange as a means of promoting trade.

Although Solon had dealt with debt in a somewhat drastic fashion, his policy by no means satisfied the party which demanded a redivision of the land. With such demands the reformer had no sympathy, as a passage from one of his poems clearly shows. Apparently he regarded debt slavery as the one evil which it was essential to destroy, and when this had been done and the farmers given a fresh start by the cancellation of mortgages, his most important task was accomplished. He took some steps, indeed, to secure the future prosperity of the poor, whether farmers or workmen, but he can hardly have expected some of these measures to have much immediate effect. He tried to develop trade and industry by inducing skilled craftsmen from other countries to settle in Athens, and he made a law that a son need not support his father if the father had not taught him a trade. We may doubt whether this law was very effective, but the motive behind it is clear. The devaluation of the drachma may have been intended to facilitate trade, as has been already pointed out. The object of another of Solon's laws is more difficult to determine. We are told that he forbade the export of any agricultural products except olive oil. This prohibition must have been aimed chiefly at grain, and it is difficult to guess what Solon's intention was. Grain would only be exported, of course, when the price abroad was higher than in Athens, and it looks as though Solon aimed at keeping down the cost of living for the benefit of the working class by preventing the farmers' taking advantage of an occasional shortage in other Greek states. If this was his purpose he may have thought that the small farmer would suffer very little loss and that it was mainly the large landowner and the speculators who benefited by such shortages. It is also possible that Solon hoped by stabilizing the price of grain at a moderately low figure to induce many farmers to turn their attention to the growing of olives rather than grain. On the whole it seems more probable that he believed he had done enough for the farmer in cancelling mortgages and felt that something must be done for the laborer as well. His policy could be defended on the ground that to allow the farmers to profit by the necessities of the laborers would impoverish the latter and give rise to bitter resentments, so that in the end the temporary gain of one class would be more than offset by the permanent loss of all.

According to Aristotle, not only had Draco reduced the customary law to writing, but he had also reorganized the government. Just what changes he made it is not easy to make out. It seems already to have passed from an aristocracy to an oligarchy in which all Athenians who could provide themselves with the equipment of a heavy-armed infantry soldier were members of the assembly. After Draco the nine archons, who were the chief magistrates, were elected by the assembly from the richest citizens. The archons held office for a year, and at the end of their term they became members of the Council of the Areopagus for life. There was also a Council of Four Hundred and One chosen by lot from the whole body of voters and apparently renewed annually. Its functions are not defined, but probably its chief, if not its only, duty was to prepare business for the assembly. In regard to the Council of the Areopagus we are informed that it acted as the guardian of the laws and supervised the magistrates to see that they obeyed them. It is also clear that the Areopagus had a wide judicial authority, for we are told that any citizen could bring a case before it by declaring what law had been broken by any injustice of which he complained. It would appear, therefore, that the Areopagites, who came exclusively from the wealthiest class, exercised a very wide control over the executive of the

state and over the administration of justice. The Four Hundred and One and the assembly, where the middle class would
predominate, seem to have played no very important part,
while the poor had no voice whatever in the government.

Such a government might in itself have been satisfactory
enough to Solon, for he was far from holding any democratic
views, but if he left it unchanged, his "new deal" would not
long survive his retirement from office. His cancellation of
debts and his freeing of the debt slaves must have caused heavy
losses to the rich and may have been disastrous to many of the
middle class. What the effect of his devaluation of the drachma
was it is difficult to say, but while it may have helped some
of the middle class, it must have injured many others. The
traders who had borrowed money on the security of ships or
goods would certainly be benefited, but their creditors lost
exactly as much as they gained. On the whole it seems possible
that a majority of the assembly was hostile to the "new deal,"
and, since the Council of Four Hundred and One was chosen
by lot from the assembly, it would almost certainly share the
views of the majority. The archons elected by the assembly
would represent the majority, and the Areopagites would be
bitterly opposed to his measures. The moment Solon was out
of the way an attack on his "new deal" was inevitable. Such
an attack might take several forms, of which the simplest would
be to repeal his measures immediately. Whether such a repeal
could be made openly retroactive we are not in a position to
say with certainty, but it would seem quite possible to make it
retroactive in fact. Probably the assembly could repeal the law
forbidding debt slavery for the future and the Council of the
Areopagus as the guardian of the laws could declare Solon's
measures illegal on the ground that he had exceeded his authority. If such open procedure was dangerous or impossible, the
courts could be employed to undo them gradually. If the law

against debt slavery were repealed, a creditor might find a
pretext to seize one of his former slaves, and, if the slave attempted to recover his freedom, the courts could refuse to
entertain his plea or could rule against him.   The archons were
the ordinary judges and were hampered by no juries, while
the only appeal from their decisions seems to have been to the
Council of the Areopagus.   Thus there was little to be hoped
for from the courts in the way of maintaining Solon's reforms.
If his measures were not flatly repealed or repudiated, the courts
were certain to regard them with hostility and to do all in their
power to evade and nullify them in particular cases.   If, therefore, Solon believed his "new deal" to be just and necessary,
he must make some changes in the constitution to safeguard
it and to secure its enforcement.   This he perceived clearly and
took steps to prevent the undoing of his work; so far as we can
judge, all his important political reforms had the defense of the
"new deal" as their primary if not their sole purpose.

In the first place, to make sure that his reforms should not
be repealed he extended the franchise so as to give even the
poorest citizen a vote.   Hitherto, as has already been said, only
those who possessed a certain property qualification had been
permitted to attend the assembly.   Those who did not have the
required amount of property were called Thetes and were
excluded from all share in the government; they were small
farmers, tenants, and farm laborers in the country, and workmen of all sorts in the city, and they greatly outnumbered the
propertied classes who alone had up to this time possessed the
franchise.   In giving the Thetes a vote Solon gave them the
potential control of the assembly, although he probably did not
anticipate that they would often attend its meetings.   During
the Peloponnesian War it was asserted that the attendance in
the assembly was rarely above 5000, perhaps a tenth of the
total number of adult citizens.   The assertion may have been

an underestimate, and, if true, the abnormal conditions during the war may have had the effect of diminishing the average attendance, but it seems probable that the statement was not far wrong and that even in peaceful times only a small fraction of the citizen body was ever present at any meeting of the assembly. We may guess that the majority of the country folk came only occasionally, since the work of their farms would often keep them at home, and, even if they could spare the time, they would not be likely to undertake a toilsome journey unless they were keenly interested in the matters likely to come up for discussion. The working class in the city and the Piraeus would be in a better position to attend, but the loss of money which an idle day involved must have deterred many from the frequent exercise of their political rights. Solon may, therefore, have thought that the propertied class would usually control the assembly. Nevertheless, the fact that the poor would henceforth have a right to come when they chose would give them a powerful negative influence. A proposal to repeal Solon's laws would now be out of the question, for such a proposal could not fail to bring them to the assembly in sufficient numbers to insure its defeat. Thus by giving the Thetes the vote Solon effectually blocked any open and direct attack upon his legislation, or at least upon any part of it in which the poor felt any serious interest.

The admission of the Thetes to the assembly necessarily gave them a voice in the election of the magistrates, and this was clearly desirable from Solon's standpoint, since it would prevent the choice of archons of violently reactionary views. He did not, however, see any reason for permitting the common people to hold office themselves, so he retained the property qualifications for all the offices and the requirement that the archons must be chosen from the wealthiest citizens. Perhaps because he regarded the Thetes with some distrust he made the election

of the archons indirect; Attica was divided into four districts
or tribes, and Solon arranged that the citizens in each tribe
should nominate ten candidates and that the nine archons
should be chosen by lot from the forty candidates so nominated.
Such, at least, is the account of Aristotle, but there are strong
reasons for suspecting his accuracy. His narrative of the events
after Solon's retirement from office seems to show that the
eponymous archon was the chief executive of the state and that
he was directly elected. It is also difficult to believe that the
lot would be allowed any part in the selection of the polemarch,
who commanded the army. Possibly these two, perhaps also
the king archon, were elected, while the other six, whose duties
were chiefly judicial, were chosen in the manner described.

In the two councils he seems to have made little, if any,
change. The ex-archons were still to be life members of the
Areopagus, and the Council of Four Hundred and One, henceforth called the Council of Four Hundred, was to be chosen
annually by lot from the propertied class, one hundred members from each tribe. The Areopagus would thus be composed
of wealthy men, while in the Four Hundred the middle class
would predominate; the Thetes would be entirely unrepre-
sented in either council. There seems from Aristotle's account
to be no truth in the often repeated statement that Solon de-
prived the Areopagus of some of its former powers. It continued to be the guardian of the laws and exercised a supervision over the most important matters. The Council of Four
Hundred seems to have had the function of preparing all
measures that were to come before the assembly, so that nothing could be initiated by the assembly itself.

It will thus be seen that, if we accept Aristotle's account, the
vote given to the Thetes had a purely negative value. They
could not bring any measure before the assembly, but could
only pass or reject such measures as were submitted by the

Council of Four Hundred. They had no voice whatever in the selection of the Four Hundred, who were chosen by lot from the propertied class. They could not directly elect any magistrate, but could merely nominate candidates from the propertied class from whom the magistrates were chosen by lot. In a direct election a man who was popular with the Thetes might easily have been elected archon, under Solon's system he could merely be chosen as one of forty candidates for the place. They could, indeed, keep any man whom they particularly disliked from getting an office, and perhaps that was as much power as Solon thought it was desirable that they should have.

To safeguard his reforms against open repeal was not enough, because it still remained possible for the judges (that is, the archons) to neutralize much of the force of his laws by ingenious interpretations, or to evade their enforcement. We cannot determine in what ways or how far his legislation could be nullified in practice, since we lack the text of the laws and know little of the procedure of that early time, but we must credit the wealthy class of Athenians, who alone could be chosen archons, with sufficient ingenuity to find pretexts of one kind or another for getting rid of measures which they bitterly resented. At any rate Solon seems to have regarded the danger as serious enough to make some sort of check on the archons necessary. The check which he devised was to set up a popular court known as the Heliaea. The exact composition of this court as organized by Solon can only be conjectured; it seems to have consisted either of all citizens over thirty years of age or else of a smaller body chosen by lot from such citizens. If all who pleased could attend the court, the Thetes could control it whenever they took the trouble to come, while, if it was chosen by lot, they would practically always be in control. It makes little difference how it was constituted, therefore, since it was certain in any case to be dominated by the poor, and we may reasonably conclude that Solon established it to give them a weapon with which they could defend themselves and their interests.

The exact powers of the popular court are as much in doubt as its composition. Two things about it, however, seem clear, namely that it could try the archons at the close of their year of office if they were charged with having abused their authority, and that it could hear appeals from the decisions of the archons. Whether any and all cases could be appealed may be doubted, but some at any rate could be, and it seems safe to assume that an appeal would be allowed if an archon attempted to enslave a man or to inflict upon him any very severe penalty. Probably Solon meant the court as a check and did not expect it to be used very frequently, since its mere existence would probably keep the archons pretty well in line. A decision which ignored or evaded Solon's laws could be at once appealed and set aside, if it entailed any serious consequences, and the archon, or archons, responsible for it could be held to strict account as soon as their term of office expired. Under such conditions Solon might feel reasonably certain that the courts would uphold and enforce his laws.

There was, however, one danger still to be guarded against. It was possible that in some cases a poor man might find himself unable to institute judicial proceedings. If a rich creditor seized him as a slave, he might be prevented from appealing to a court until he had been sold to a slave trader and taken out of the country. Moreover, since many of the rich nobles were very powerful, the poor might sometimes think it safer to suffer injustice than to resist it. To meet such difficulties Solon decreed that anyone who had knowledge of a wrong might bring an action, whereas hitherto this could be done only by those who were actually injured. By thus extending the right of prosecution Solon might hope to enlist all who sympathized with his measures in the task of enforcing them.

In after times Solon was naturally regarded as the founder of democracy in Athens and Aristotle views him from this standpoint, pointing out as the three most democratic features of his reforms the abolition of debt slavery, the extension of the right to prosecute to anyone who knew of a wrong which had been committed, and the institution of the popular court. At first we may feel some surprise at the failure of the great philosopher to include the admission of the Thetes to the assembly, but it must be remembered that if Aristotle is right in regard to the method of choosing the archons, the right to attend the assembly had an almost purely negative value. Even if they attended its meetings regularly and in large numbers, the assembly possessed no power of initiative and could only pass or reject the measures submitted to it by the Council of Four Hundred, a body in the selection of which the Thetes had no voice whatever. In the popular court, however, they could exert a constant pressure on the magistrates because of their right to try them at the close of their term of office. In his *Politics* (ii, 12) Aristotle adds that the judicial power of the people made it necessary to flatter them and contributed to make the government a pure democracy. He says also that some persons blamed Solon for establishing the popular court, since by doing so he created an institution which would soon overthrow the constitutional balance at which he aimed. Such a view assumes that Solon's political reforms were a thing apart from his economic reforms and were undertaken for their own sake. That men of a later generation should hold such a view is natural enough, but it is possible that the assumption is wholly wrong and that Solon was not interested in political reforms in themselves but was seeking simply to protect his "new deal" against his opponents. Certainly he made no attempt to take the control of the government out of the hands of the propertied class or to give the poor a serious voice in it. Even if we assume that two or three of the archons were elected by direct vote of the assembly, we may doubt whether the poor gained much by being allowed to participate. These archons had charge of the executive, war, and religious matters and must always come from the wealthy class. Neither the conduct of war nor matters of religion were likely to cause party divisions, and if the populace were able to keep re- actionaries out of the executive, it may not have seemed a very important power to Solon nor a thing to be regretted. We may be sure that a popular court trying *all* cases and an assembly controlling the entire government were things of which he never even dreamed. In one of his poems he declares that he gave the common people sufficient privileges without permitting the upper classes to suffer any indignity. Evidently his aim was not a democracy but an oligarchy in which the people should have just enough power to maintain his economic re- forms and to protect themselves against oppression by their rulers.

Solon made many other reforms of which we can judge very imperfectly. He revised the code of Draco and seems to have yielded to the temptation which always besets reformers to improve the morals and manners of the people by legislation; in particular he attempted to regulate funerals and women. It is unlikely that in regard to women he was more successful than other male reformers have been since his day. Although he doubtless exaggerated the part which laws can play in human life, he did introduce a milder criminal law, and, if we had fuller information in regard to his code, we should probably find that his "new deal" was by no means limited to the measures which we have here considered.

The actual success of the "new deal" is difficult to determine on account of our scanty information. It seems certain, however, that it accomplished much; debt slavery was definitely and finally destroyed, and Solon's reforms seem to have been followed by a period of slowly increasing prosperity. To what extent this prosperity was due to Solon we cannot undertake to say with certainty. If he had freed the farmers from their debts, he had done little, if anything, to enable them to keep out of debt in the future. His work roused very general discontent at the moment, since he had gone too far to please some and not far enough to please others. After he laid down his office, the strife of parties began again, as bitter and violent as ever, and in the end the distracted state was quieted by a dictatorship. A kinsman of Solon, Pisistratus by name, posing as the champion of the poor, succeeded in making himself tyrant of Athens (560 B.C.). Pisistratus, however, was a statesman of real ability, who consolidated and supplemented Solon's work. To relieve the pressure on the land he gave employment to the poor by undertaking public works and encouraging trade and industry. Since his enemies were to be found chiefly among the wealthy landowners, he drove many of them into exile, confiscating their estates and dividing them among the poor. To help the small farmers in their difficulties he loaned money to them at a low rate of interest. Perhaps this policy had as its principal object to enable many of them to turn to other crops than grain. Solon may have tried to promote the cultivation of the olive by law, but Pisistratus followed a more practical course. Apparently it was not until the time of the Tyranny that grapes began to be grown in Attica. Probably the loans of Pisistratus made it possible for many small landowners to transform their farms into vineyards. This was difficult for the farmer whose land barely supported him, because the vines required more than a year to mature and he had somehow to live until they began to bear. A loan at low interest might tide him over the interval, and once the vineyard became productive the profits would be much greater than could be made by raising grain on the same land. Moreover, much of Attica was ill adapted to grain, but was admirably suited to grapes and olives. With the spread of these cultures and the breaking up of some of the large estates many of the poorer farmers became prosperous and contented, while the public works of Pisistratus and the expanding commerce of Athens, resulting from the changes in agriculture and the growing industries, which the tyrant did what he could to foster, relieved the pressure on the land by providing other occupations for the surplus peasantry. In after times we are told that men looked back to the days of the Tyranny as a golden age when wages were high and work abundant. Pisistratus no doubt gained more credit than he deserved; he inherited the results of Solon's "new deal," which he expanded and developed intelligently, but one or two men cannot make prosperity. The greatest service of Solon was, perhaps, that his measures averted a violent explosion which might have ruined Athens, while Pisistratus put an end to political instability and confusion which were a serious obstacle in the way of the economic forces whose operation finally made Athens prosperous.

II

UNEMPLOYMENT AND IMPERIALISM

It was one of the misfortunes of the ancient world that prosperity inevitably produced unemployment. This was due to the institution of slavery. At first a period of economic activity and expansion created an increased demand for labor and provided the poor with work at reasonable wages, but, if such a period lasted for any length of time, it naturally resulted in the accumulation of capital, which demanded profitable investment. In so far as the newly accumulated capital was invested in business it was likely to be used for the purchase of slaves, who replaced the free laborers hitherto employed in production. The obvious result was that free men found the jobs open to them diminishing in number, and those who continued to work were forced to do so in competition with slave labor. In brief, then, prosperity in ancient times did not end with a depression followed by a more or less rapid and complete recovery, but gradually threw the poor out of work and ended by producing a larger or smaller class which was permanently unemployed. Every ancient state, therefore, after a period of prosperity found itself faced with serious political and social problems. How it would attempt to solve these problems depended in part upon its form of government and in part upon the circumstances under which the solution was undertaken. In a democracy the poor were certain, sooner or later, to try to find some relief from their growing poverty by using their control of the government for this purpose. But the action of the government, whatever form it might take,

would in the end cost money, which, unless the state was so
situated that it could put the burden on others, would have to
be raised by the taxation of its own propertied class. If the
state had an oligarchical government, the propertied class could,
indeed, refrain from taxing themselves if they were strong
enough to feel confident that they could deal successfully with
any attempts at revolution. In many of the ancient city states
this was likely to be the case, for, although the poor were always
more numerous than the rich, the propertied class were far
better armed and trained than their potential opponents. In
such states an oligarchy may be said to be the natural form of
government, the overthrow of which required some form of
outside interference. It was only in states where the navy was
of vital importance that democracy had a secure basis, since
it was the poor who manned the ships as sailors and rowers
just as the propertied class composed the heavy infantry in
the army.

If Athens became prosperous under Pisistratus, the reaction
was certain to be felt in time, and another "new deal" would
sooner or later be demanded. In point of fact this actually
happened, but the second "new deal" took a form which has
to a great degree concealed its real character, for this second
"new deal" was neither more nor less than the Athenian
Empire. A brief examination of the Empire from this point of
view may be of interest and may throw some light upon the
policy of Athens.

The overthrow of the Tyranny in Athens (510 B.C.) was
brought about by the intervention of Sparta and was followed
by a reorganization of the government by Cleisthenes. It
may be doubted whether he made the institutions of Athens
more democratic, as is often said, but he certainly rendered
them more efficient. He seems to have given the common
people no more power than they had received from Solon, but

he broke up the old political parties, gave the middle class a more active role in the government, and may have done much to teach the poor how to make use of the privileges which they already had by appealing to them for support in carrying his reforms.

Not long after his work was completed, Athens and all Greece had to confront the Persian invasion. The first attack of the Persians was met and defeated by Athens at Marathon (490 B.C.), and for a time the danger seemed to have passed. Perhaps only a few of the more clear-sighted among her statesmen realized that the Great King had not accepted the verdict of this battle as final and that he was actively engaged in preparing a new expedition. In fact, circumstances, together with the extent of the necessary preparations, gave Athens a breathing spell of ten years, and during this period a vitally important change took place in her policy. The political leaders were now Aristides and Themistocles, who soon became rivals. The treasury had unexpectedly acquired a large surplus, owing to the discovery of rich veins of silver in mines owned by the state, and Aristides advocated the distribution of this surplus among the citizens. Such a measure would possibly have resulted in strengthening the army, at least to some extent, by enabling some of the Thetes to provide themselves with the arms and armor for service in the heavy infantry. Themistocles proposed instead of such a distribution to use the money for building a large number of new triremes for the navy, and in the end his policy was adopted. A war with Aegina, which was then going on, no doubt aided Themistocles, but his policy seems to have gone far beyond the immediate needs of this war. What arguments he used we have no means of knowing, and we can only guess at the motives which swayed the assembly. If, however, we assume that the prosperity which had marked the period of the Tyranny was passing and that the poor were beginning to feel the effects of an increase in slave labor, it is possible to explain his victory with some plausibility. At first glance a distribution of money would seem to be a bait calculated to secure the support of the poor for his rival, but his policy would also make a strong appeal to them, because the building and manning of the new ships would provide more or less permanent employment for a considerable number, and there might be many who would prefer a steady job to an immediate, but not very large, bonus and the prospect of a small pension for some years to come. Whatever the causes may have been, Themistocles was successful and his policy made Athens the strongest naval power in Greece. Whether he realized it or not, in persuading the Athenians to place their reliance on their fleet rather than their army, he committed Athens to the development of her nascent democracy and laid the foundation for her future Empire.

The expansion of the fleet had hardly been completed when Xerxes led the Persian hosts to the conquest of Greece (480 B.C.). The events of the struggle need not detain us; it will suffice to point out that the increase in the Athenian fleet was the most important single factor in the salvation of Greece. When the Persians had been successfully driven from the mainland of Europe, the Greeks had inevitably to consider their future security, for they had no means of knowing whether Xerxes would abandon his ambitious plans, or whether, like his father, he would begin preparations for another attempt. The best security attainable under the circumstances was to be found in continuing an aggressive campaign against the Persians until they had been completely expelled from the Aegean and the coast cities of Asia Minor had been liberated from their rule. For the leadership of such a campaign Sparta was obviously unfitted, and it was only natural that she and many of the states of the peninsula should drop out of the war

as soon as all immediate danger to Greece itself seemed to have
been averted. Those states, however, which felt a keener
interest in the war, because they were likely to be the first
victims of any new attack, determined to persevere and proceeded to organize the Confederacy of Delos with Athens as
their leader.

The new role which Athens was thus called upon to play
was one which she was very ready to assume, indeed it was
one which she could not well have declined even had she
wished. There seems little doubt that her population was
already too numerous to subsist upon the food which could be
produced in Attica and that she was now importing a considerable part of her grain. The best source of supply was the
region around the Black Sea, both because it was easily acces-
sible and because she could find there a ready market for her
olive oil, wine, and manufactured goods. But her trade with
this region would always be liable to sudden and disastrous
interruption as long as Persia was allowed to retain any foothold in the Aegean. It is not easy to determine to what extent
the governments of the ancient city states were influenced by
commercial or economic interests of a general sort, but the provision of an adequate food supply was a matter which could not
be ignored. Motives of a very pressing kind, therefore, urged
Athens to continue the war and to rally around her all the
other Greek states whom she could induce to accept her leadership, so that the Confederacy of Delos was the natural consequence of the defeat of Xerxes. That idealistic motives were
combined with material ones is undoubtedly true, for few
enterprises would make a stronger appeal to Greek sentiment
than a war to liberate their brother Greeks from the rule of the
barbarian, and the force of such an appeal was in no wise
weakened by the fact that such liberation was the most effective
safeguard against future dangers. The result was that many

of the Greek states entered with zeal upon the task of clearing
the Aegean of the Persians, and Athens became the leader of a
formidable confederacy (477 B.C.). In accepting the leadership of Athens the other states in no way dreamed of placing
themselves under her control, and in the beginning the Confederacy was a confederacy in fact as well as in name, but this
condition was not destined to endure for long. The success
of the Confederacy was rapid and brilliant, and with the attainment of the primary purpose of the alliance a crisis came.
Naxos, apparently feeling that the existence of the Confederacy
was no longer necessary, decided to secede and resume its
former independence. If this were permitted, either the entire
Confederacy would soon break up or those who considered its
continuance essential to their safety would have to bear greatly
augmented burdens. It might be argued that if it broke up
Persia would promptly attempt to recover some part at least
of what she had just lost and to regain a foothold in the Aegean.
If it were answered that in this case the Confederacy could be
reorganized at once, the reply was obvious from some of the
states that it would be precisely their capture by the Persians
which would give the warning to the others. Athens, apparently with the support of most of the other members, re-
solved that the Confederacy must be maintained and compelled
Naxos to remain by force (ca. 468 B.C.). Henceforth the
Confederacy was no longer a free league of states, but contained a class of unwilling or subject members, which class
rapidly increased in number. As it grew, the control of Athens
over her allies tightened until in a comparatively short time
the Confederacy disappeared in all but name and was replaced
by an Athenian Empire.

If we ignore details and look only at the broad outlines of
the transformation, the process will seem a natural and inevitable one. Persia could be driven out of the Aegean and

kept out only by a combination of the city states in that region, since no one of them and no small group of them possessed the resources for the task. A confederation in which all the members should have an effective voice in the management of affairs was only possible if the states would voluntarily coöperate in the common task. As soon as some of them refused to bear their share of the burden, the independence of the members was doomed. If the Confederacy broke up, they would be reconquered by Persia, and it could only be held together if the strongest state among them assumed control. It is impossible to believe that Athens had originally any imperialistic designs, although it is of course conceivable that some individual Athenians had. The course of events, however, soon taught the leading city lessons which her people were not slow to learn. Since continuance of the Confederacy was a necessity for Athens, she was prepared to take any steps necessary to hold it together, and experience soon convinced her that it could be held together only by reducing her allies to the condition of subject states.

It has already been suggested that the safety of the Athenian food supply required that the Hellespont should be guarded against the possibility of Persian attack and that the best means of accomplishing this result was by driving Persia completely out of the Aegean. From an attack by land the cities on the Hellespont could be protected by fortifications, and what Athens had chiefly to dread was an attack by sea, which might cut off her communications with the Greek colonies on the coast of the Black Sea. Such an attack was impossible if Persia had neither ships nor naval bases in the Aegean, but, if the Confederacy fell to pieces, Persia might recover some of the cities on the coast of Asia Minor and some of the islands, and so regain both. The safety of the Athenian food supply, therefore, was involved in the maintenance of the Confederacy, but

there were other ways in which her interests were almost
equally involved. It is highly probable that the Athenian
working class were feeling the competition of slave labor before
the Persian wars. The naval program of Themistocles and
the maritime expeditions in the first years of the Confederacy
undoubtedly gave employment to many of the poorer citizens.
At any rate it is certain that the fleet required the services of
many citizens as sailors and rowers, for slaves were not used
in either capacity until the Peloponnesian War and then only
because enough free men could not be found. It is difficult to
believe that if work at good wages was easy to find in Athens
her citizens would have been willing to quit their jobs ashore
to become rowers in a trireme. The fact that Athens expe-
rienced no difficulty in manning her ships seems to show that
the condition of the working class was becoming such that the
fleet offered a welcome alternative. Yet it is obvious that the
more the poor relied on the fleet for a living, the more indispensable the fleet became, for the withdrawal of citizens from
other work for naval service must have had a tendency to
foster the employment of slave labor. Any serious reduction
of the fleet, therefore, would leave many men without work
and with less chance than ever of obtaining it. But the fleet
of Athens had grown steadily in size and was in part maintained by the treasury of the Confederacy.

When the Confederacy was formed, some of the states had
agreed to furnish ships to the allied fleet, while others had
preferred to pay a sum of money instead. How the money
was used we are not informed in detail, but it is easy to conjecture how it might have been. It seems probable that those
states which furnished ships also supplied and paid the crew,
but that the fleet thus provided for was not large enough for
the purpose. If such were the case, it would be natural to pay
over the money to such states as had extra ships and men on

condition that they send a larger contingent than their obligations to the Confederacy called for. Since it was with Athens
chiefly, if not solely, that such arrangements were made, the
result was that her navy was supported to a considerable extent
by the Confederate treasury. Although the details here suggested are conjectural, we do at least know that this general
result was arrived at in some fashion and that as time went on
Athens drew more and more largely on the tribute of the allies.
To some extent this was their own fault, for many which had
at first contributed ships voluntarily substituted a money
payment, and this of course forced the Confederacy to find the
ships elsewhere. The tribute of the allies in the end made it
possible for Athens to maintain a fleet far stronger than she
could have done out of her own revenues, and the possession of
this fleet made it more and more easy for her to impose her
will on her allies and left them more and more completely
helpless against her. Under such conditions discontent was
inevitable, and with discontent came measures of precaution
and a steadily increasing control of the allies by their former
leader, so that they soon ceased to be allies in anything but
name and became in fact subjects of an imperial city. Not that
Athens ever attempted to govern them directly or thought of
doing so; each retained its own separate and distinct government and managed its own affairs, Athens contenting herself
with regulating and controlling the action of these governments
within certain definite and specified limits. The limits, however, were defined by Athens, and they were specified in
treaties which she dictated to each separate ally. Nominally,
of course, the treaty was a voluntary agreement between the
two parties, but actually it must often have been drawn up by
Athens with little left to the ally except to sign on the dotted
line. Nevertheless the treaty was the legal base on which the
relations between the two rested, and the method of separate

treaties with each ally had the advantage of leaving Athens
free to vary the precise terms according to her view of what
was advantageous or necessary in each case. In general the
ally delegated to Athens the control of certain matters, and
was promised certain rights and privileges in return. Powers
not expressly delegated were doubtless retained by the local
government, although the ally would in most cases be quite
helpless to resist if Athens chose to encroach or if she sometimes
forgot the limits which she had herself set to her control.

In its original form the Confederacy was governed by a
congress in which each state had an equal voice, so that Athens
could not impose her will unless she was able to secure the
voluntary support of a majority of the allies. Such support,
however, soon ceased to be necessary, for as the power of Athens
grew the decisions of the congress mattered less and less until
the will of Athens alone was of any practical importance, since
she had come to possess in her fleet the means to carry out her
will regardless of the feelings of her allies. The meetings of
the congress, therefore, became a mere matter of form and at
length were altogether discontinued. When this happened, all
disguise had been abandoned and Athens stood forth openly as
an imperial power, a city state ruling some two hundred other
city states. Such a transformation of the Confederacy may
have been a tragedy, but it was in no way the peculiar fault
of Athens. The fatal defect of the Greek race throughout its
history was its inability to achieve any sort of stable and voluntary union. The city state was its characteristic form of political
organization, and no combination of such states would long
endure except under external pressure. For defense against
aggression the states might and did unite in leagues, but, when
the danger had been averted, these leagues always displayed a
strong tendency to dissolve into their original elements, a
tendency which could only be checked by force, and the use

of force led straight to some form of imperialism. Perhaps the chief cause of this rooted particularism of the Greeks lay in the structure of their city states, and a brief examination of the case of Athens may serve to throw some light on the obstacles in the way of any organic union among them.

It has often been pointed out that none of the Greek city states was capable of any serious expansion except in an imperialistic sense, that is to say, one city state might rule others but it could not absorb them. This is true enough, but the nature of the difficulty has not been clearly perceived. As a result Athens has frequently been blamed for her treatment of her allies on the assumption that she might have pursued a more liberal and generous policy toward them. To demand any other policy than that actually adopted, however, is to demand that the Athenian democracy should commit suicide. Some of her critics have held that she should have preserved the congress of the Confederacy and sought to construct a genuine federal government. It seems obvious, however, that the congress could only be used for such a purpose if it was entrusted with some real power, and that this was possible only if the allies would voluntarily work in harmony with Athens. If the allies were discontented and unwilling to coöperate, any powers which the congress might retain would be used to hamper the work of the Confederacy and ultimately to disrupt it. When Naxos was forced to remain in the Confederacy and to continue her contributions to a common cause in which she no longer felt any vital interest, it seems clear that if she were allowed to retain a vote in the congress she would have employed it only to obstruct the will of the loyal allies and to promote dissensions among them. If the Confederacy was to be maintained, it was necessary to curb disruptive tendencies, and those states which required a curb could not be allowed a voice in the matter.

When discontent became more or less general among the allies, Athens could not preserve the congress unless she were sure of dominating it on all matters of importance, and in that case nothing of real value was to be gained by its preservation, since no state was likely to be reconciled by being consulted under such conditions that it was certain to have no influence on the decision. The use of force, therefore, to hold the Confederacy together was bound in the end to reduce the congress to a nullity unless the states against which it was necessary to use force were comparatively few in number. Athens would seem to have had only the alternatives of letting the Confederacy go to pieces or of abolishing the congress and taking control into her own hands.

Another criticism frequently made is that, if Athens could not make a real federation out of the Confederacy, she should have pursued a liberal policy toward her subject allies and encouraged them to look forward to the time when they might be absorbed in the dominant state by acquiring Athenian citizenship. Here the contrast between Athens and Rome has often been pointed out, and Roman statesmanship extolled in contrast to Athenian shortsighted selfishness. The circumstances, however, were essentially different and rendered the course pursued by Rome impossible for Athens. The fundamental difference lay in the fact that Athens was a real democracy, while Rome was not. In the Roman assembly the vote was taken by groups instead of by individuals and the voting groups were so organized that a minority of the citizens present was practically certain always to control the decision. In the Athenian assembly, on the other hand, the vote was taken by individuals and the will of a majority of those present was certain to prevail. This fact made any serious extension of citizenship a very real danger to the democracy, nor is it difficult to see why this was the case.

In theory the Athenian assembly was composed of all Athenian citizens, but in practice it was, of course, composed of that fraction of the citizen body which chose, or was able, to attend any given meeting. Whatever the number, those present were treated as the people and the absent were ignored. Now there is strong reason to think that the actual attendance was usually comparatively small, and that, out of a total of some 50,000 citizens, there were seldom present at a meeting of the assembly more than five or six thousand. Even if this be something of an underestimate, it is clear that a large proportion of the citizens could seldom attend, for many of the country folk lived so far from Athens that the journey to the city was too laborious to be readily undertaken, and further both the small farmers and the working class were in the main too much occupied with the business of getting a living to spare the time to attend frequently, even when the demands of their employment did not make attendance impossible. The farmer could not leave his work in certain seasons without grave risk of serious loss, and the sailor or rower in the fleet was necessarily absent from the city during a considerable part of the year. The assembly, therefore, consisted in practice of those citizens who were sufficiently interested in politics and were otherwise so situated as to be able and willing to attend. It is evident that men of some property who resided in the city itself were in a better position to attend regularly than were the urban poor or the farmers, and that, therefore, the political influence of the propertied class was much greater than their number in the total citizen body would entitle them to claim. Not only might such a result be expected *a priori*, but a survey of Athenian history shows that it was actually the case. There were in general two major parties in Athens, which we may call the Democrats and the Conservatives. The Democrats, though led by men of wealth and often of aristocratic birth, relied in the main upon the support of the poor, while the propertied class as a whole were on the side of the Conservatives. Since in all human societies the poor greatly outnumber the more fortunate classes, a system of representative government would have placed the Democrats securely in power in Athens, unless the country folk aligned themselves with the Conservatives. With the assembly constituted as it was, the Democrats predominated during the greater part of the time, but their predominance was often somewhat precarious. Even the most popular of the Democratic leaders found the opposition so strong at times that their supremacy was more or less in danger, and it was this circumstance that gave the institution of ostracism its real use and value.

Whatever may have been the purpose for which Cleisthenes originally devised ostracism, it was ultimately employed by the Democratic leaders to free themselves from rivals who, though not supported by a majority of the people, were yet strong enough in the assembly to make it difficult for the majority to ensure the carrying out of the policy which they had more or less definitely endorsed. In this connection it must be remembered that a single vote of the assembly was never sufficient to settle any important question of policy. The decrees of the people were always comparatively short and dealt with only one matter at a time. If the assembly had attempted to pass long and complicated bills, it would have found itself unable to act intelligently on the questions before it and democratic government would have been little more than a farce. This fact, however, meant that in practice it was only possible to carry out any policy if its advocates could secure the passing of a number of successive decrees at different meetings of the assembly. Such a result was not always easy to secure, because the assembly was a very fluctuating body, varying greatly in size and composition from one meeting to another, and the parties, at least during the period of Athenian greatness, were somewhat loosely organized and were little more than the personal followers of some prominent politician. Under such conditions there was not only a possibility but at times a real danger that, after a leader had induced the assembly at one meeting to sanction some part of his program, this action would be practically nullified by the defeat of some other part at a subsequent meeting when the attendance happened to be somewhat unusual either in number or in character, or the rival leader happened to make an exceptionally eloquent speech. Moreover, it is unlikely that all those who attended the assembly had a clear conception of a policy as a whole. It might easily happen that at a particular meeting there were present a large number of citizens who had not heard the discussion at previous meetings and who judged the measure before the assembly without reference to other measures already passed. A statesman, therefore, however popular he might be in a general way and however great the confidence which the majority of the citizens had in him, might find real difficulty in making his policy effective if he was faced by a strong opposition under an able leader, even though this opposition came from a minority of the whole citizen body. Historians have seldom realized these difficulties and have generally assumed that when Themistocles had persuaded the Athenian assembly to pass a decree devoting the surplus in the treasury to the building of ships the whole question was settled, but this was far from being the case. The building of the ships was only a beginning, and it was necessary to secure the passing of other decrees at subsequent meetings to provide for equipping and manning the ships after they were built. There was, therefor, a real motive for the ostracism of Aristides, because his absence would greatly increase the chances that Themistocles would be able to carry out his policy. This was true not

merely because it would remove Aristides from the scene, but
even more because without him as a leader his followers were
likely to be so disorganized and discouraged that their opposition would be futile if they did not abandon it altogether.
That the institution had a real use in this way is made
abundantly clear by the incoherent and confused action of the
assembly at a later period when ostracism had become obsolete.
Why the institution was permitted to disappear is a question
calling for some better explanation than has usually been given;
we may surmise that it was due in large part to a better organization of parties, which made the removal of a single leader far
less effective than in the earlier period. At any rate such an
explanation is suggested by what we are told of the ostracism
of Hyperbolus in 417 B.C., the last ostracism held.

The fluctuating and uncertain character of the assembly not
only gave ostracism its value, but it had other consequences as
well. Although the Democrats had normally a majority in the
assembly, it was a somewhat precarious one and by no means
corresponded to their predominance among the citizens. Under
such conditions the extension of citizenship to the allies might
easily have upset the party balance in Athens, and have paved
the way, perhaps, for the overthrow of the Athenian democracy
altogether. It is obvious that if citizenship were conferred upon
the Naxians, for example, the poorer class among the new
citizens would be unable to come to Athens to attend the meetings of the assembly; those who did come would belong almost
exclusively to the wealthy class and would thus simply serve
to increase the strength of the Conservative opposition. If
citizenship was extended widely enough among the allies to be
of any use in reconciling them to their position, it would endanger the control of the assembly by the Democrats of Athens.
Such a result may not seem to us a particularly bad thing, since
the Conservatives might have guided the policy of Athens with

better ultimate success than did the Democrats, and in any case they could hardly have ruined Athens more completely. Such a view, however, is one which we cannot expect that the Democrats would take.

Moreover, there was another phase of the matter which the Democrats had to consider. During most of Athenian history both parties and all classes did outward homage to the democratic constitution of the state, and no man taking part in public life could venture any open attack upon it, but the appearance of unanimity did not mean that real unanimity existed. It is obvious from many signs that the poor regarded the propertied class as a whole with a good deal of distrust, suspecting that in their hearts they would have been glad to set up an oligarchy in place of the existing form of government, and their conduct after the Sicilian disaster seems to show that this suspicion was not without a foundation in fact. The Athenian Democrats might, therefore, feel that, if the propertied class secured a reliable majority in the assembly, it would no longer be a question merely of the wisest policy to pursue but a matter of grave doubt whether the fundamental institutions of the state could be preserved. If the poor ceased to control the assembly, it would become legally possible to disfranchise them altogether, and the only real protection against an oligarchy would be a resort to force. The extension of citizenship to the subject allies would thus not only endanger the immediate supremacy of the Democrats in Athens, but ultimately the Athenian democracy itself. The result might, indeed, turn out to be even worse than this, for it was by no means certain that the extension of citizenship to the allies would make any serious difference in their feelings; if the Athenians tried the experiment, they might have discovered too late that they had wrecked their own form of government without diminishing the discontent of their subjects. It should be borne in mind that experience was to prove that an oligarchic Sparta was no more successful than a democratic Athens in holding together a large number of city states.

It seems clear, then, that a city state of the Athenian type could not expand beyond very narrow limits without incurring the risk of self-destruction. The same thing was in some degree true of the other city states of Greece. Even for a state with an oligarchical form of government indefinite expansion was impossible. If too much territory was included in the state, a large proportion of its citizens were unable to take any part in its political life, and the result was practically the same as an avowed imperialism. If an oligarchy had been established in Athens and if after conquering Boeotia it had tried to incorporate Thebes, the result would have been unsatisfactory from both sides. The well-to-do Thebans might vote by going to Athens, but they could hardly be expected to do so very often, and, when they were absent, the government dominated by the Athenian oligarchs might repeal all the measures passed while they were present. In fact they could hardly attend meetings in Athens regularly enough to have any serious influence, and to all intents and purposes Thebes would be ruled by Athens. It is unlikely that the barren name of citizens would reconcile the Thebans to such a condition. As long as the Greeks clung to direct instead of representative government, the citizens who resided in the capital were bound to control the state. If the state expanded beyond definite and narrow limits, the result in practice was that one city state ruled over a number of others which were too far away to have a real voice in the government but were able under certain circumstances to be a disturbing influence in politics.

In her imperialistic policy Athens followed the only course open to her unless she was prepared to allow members of the Confederacy of Delos to withdraw from it at any time they

chose, trusting that enough of them would voluntarily remain
to make it possible to keep Persia out of the Aegean. Probably
no state, ancient or modern, would have taken the risks involved in the second alternative, and we can hardly blame
Athens for rejecting it. The risks would have been not merely
external from Persia but internal as well. The Confederacy
had solved for Athens, temporarily at least, any problem of
unemployment which she may have had at home. Even if we
assume that when the Confederacy was formed the problem
had not yet arisen, the work of the Confederacy in the war
against Persia had called into service a large number of
Athenian citizens, whose places at home must have been filled
in some fashion. To demobilize the large fleet maintained by
the tribute of the allies would have immediately created an
unemployment problem of serious dimensions. No class or
party in Athens could be blind to so obvious a result or was
likely to face the responsibility if it could be avoided. For
many and imperative reasons it was necessary for Athens to
prevent the disintegration of the Confederacy, even if this
required its transformation into an Athenian Empire. The
longer the Empire lasted the larger the number of Athenian
citizens who depended upon it for their daily bread. This fact
explains why the Democrats in Athens were the extreme im-
perialists, while the Conservatives were inclined to modera-
tion. Not that the propertied class was opposed to imperialism
—its advantages to them, if only in giving work to the poor, were
too obvious for that—but they were disposed to hold what they
had rather than to seek further expansion and to avoid pressing Athenian control over the subject allies farther than was
necessary. To the poor, on the other hand, the Empire not
only gave employment, but any expansion of it might be expected to improve their condition to some extent.

What proportion of the poorer citizens of Athens relied upon the Empire for their living it is impossible to compute with accuracy, but enough is known to show something of the conditions that existed. The fleet furnished work for a very considerable number as sailors and rowers, although by no means all who served in this way were citizens, for we know that both metics and foreigners were hired. We do not know with certainty just how many ships were on active duty in time of peace; if Plutarch (*Pericles*, xi, 4) is well informed, Pericles to secure his hold on the assembly sent out a squadron of sixty ships and kept them at sea for eight months of the year. Such a squadron would require from 10,000 to 12,000 rowers and sailors, not to count officers and marines, most of whom were probably citizens if Plutarch is correct as to his purpose. In addition to these, the popular courts in Athens, if they were all ten in session at once, as seems to have been usually the case, would require 5,000 jurors, who were paid for their services. How these jurors were selected is not perfectly clear, but, whatever the method of choosing them, the result seems to have been that jury service became a sort of old age pension. There were apparently many citizens who in their youth earned their living in some form of active employment, and when too old for this supported themselves by serving as jurors. Even if we estimate the number employed on the fleet and in the juries at only 10,000, the number is very large when we remember that the total number of Athenian citizens was only 50,000 to 55,000 at the most. Of course without the Empire Athens would have had a fleet and courts, but she certainly could not have maintained her fleet on the scale she did without the tribute of the allies, and the courts would have had much less to do if cases had not been brought before them on appeal from all over the Empire. The loss of the Empire would have meant a sharp curtailment of activity in both directions and so would

have been a direct menace to the incomes of a very considerable
proportion of the Athenian citizen body. Such direct employment was, however, only a part of the matter. Whatever the
number of ships which Athens sent out each year on active
service, she had a large number of others in reserve at the
Piraeus. All these had to be built and kept in repair, equipment in the shape of ropes and sails had to be provided, and
these necessities must have given employment to many. Then,
too, Pericles initiated and carried out an extensive program of
public works, openly paid for out of the tribute of the allies,
which must have given employment to many citizens, although
many of the laborers were metics and slaves. Last of all,
Athens adopted the practice of planting colonies of her poor
citizens among her allies, which must have provided for a
considerable number. Such an enumeration is by no means
complete, even for our limited knowledge, and all fields where
the propertied class were likely to enter into the calculation
have been omitted, but it seems a safe guess that somewhat
more than a fifth of the Athenian citizens were more or less
directly dependent on the Empire for a livelihood, and those
who were not could hardly avoid seeing that serious consequences to themselves must follow the throwing out of work
of so large a number.

It seems clear, therefore, that a policy of imperialism was
forced upon Athens by the conditions both at home and abroad.
Once the Empire was formed she had little choice but to hold
it firmly by every available means. What some of these
means were is worth a moment's examination, as well as the
reaction which they provoked among the allies. The basis of
her power was of course her fleet, but besides this engine of
direct force she was able to apply pressure in other ways. The
control of the Hellespont was necessary to ensure her own
food supply, but this control gave her an obvious means of

holding in line all states of the Empire which relied to any
important extent on the grain of the Black Sea region. How
many states there were which like Athens lived largely on
imported food we cannot determine, but there must have been
some, perhaps many, whose dependence on such food was great
enough to make them think very seriously before they ven-
tured to defy a power able to cut them off from all access to
the most convenient source of supply. In the same way the
fleet of Athens gave her control over the commerce of her
allies, and many must have been very reluctant to risk a
blockade or an embargo shutting them out of the ports of the
other allies. The economic pressure which Athens could thus
apply was probably as effective a force in holding the Empire
together as her military or naval power. It was also easy for
Athens to take precautions against revolt. In some of her
subject allies she could and did insist on the destruction of all
walls and fortifications. This, however, was only possible
where her navy was an adequate protection for the ally; where
this was not the case and fortifications were needed as a defense
against other possible enemies, she might station a garrison in
the citadel, nominally as an added safeguard to the ally. Then,
too, those states where colonies of Athenian citizens had been
settled found that these colonies, although not of a military
character, yet performed some of the functions of a garrison.
When we take account of these precautions and recall that
none of the subject allies had a navy, it will be seen that they
were practically helpless to resist the dominant city.

Yet it was not by force and fear solely that Athens maintained her Empire or kept her subject allies in obedience. By
constituting herself the champion and protector of democracy
she was able to bind many of her allies to her by strong ties
of interest if not of affection. It is highly probable that many

of the city states which combined to form the Confederacy of Delos already had democratic governments, and in many others Athens found an opportunity or seized upon some pretext to set up a democracy in place of the oligarchy which had previously been in power. In pursuing this policy she was actuated not only by a natural sympathy for this form of government, but also by a clear perception of her own interest. It has already been pointed out that owing to the fact that the propertied class was better armed than the poor, a democracy in many of the Greek city states was certain to prove an unstable government incapable of maintaining itself without outside support. Where this was the case, a democracy, if once established, would of necessity be faithful to the power from which it received such support. In many of the subject allies it must have been true that a rebellion against Athens would have meant a domestic revolution, and in such states the mass of the people had no choice but to be loyal to Athens or to submit to the rule of the local oligarchs. As the champion of democracy Athens was thus able to secure a popular basis for her Empire and to enlist the majority of the population on her side. To many of her subjects her rule appeared less as an alien tyranny than as a guaranty of freedom and an effective protection against oppression.

There was, of course, another side to the picture. In winning the active loyalty, or the passive support, of the masses, Athens incurred the bitter resentment of the oligarchic party. In their eyes she was responsible not only for all her own sins but also for all those of the democracies of which she made herself the protector. To them the overthrow of Athenian control was a necessary preliminary to the overthrow of their opponents at home. It is often said that the Greeks were so deeply attached to the ideal of the absolute autonomy of each city state that

they submitted only with extreme reluctance to any abridg-
ment of it, but the recorded facts of their history furnish comparatively little support for such a view. It would be truer to
say that the strife of parties in the Greek states was so bitter
that each party was ready, if necessary, to sacrifice the independence of the state to secure its own supremacy.

The cause of this bitterness is no doubt to be sought in the
economic situation in many of the states. If some repetition be
permitted, as long as slavery remained an accepted institution,
a period of prosperity was bound to be followed by a period
of increasing hardship for the laboring class, who would naturally see in some form of state intervention the best, if not
the only, means of improving their condition. If they were
able to control the government, they were practically certain to
use their power for this purpose, and in most cases the propertied class would be obliged to pay the bills. A democracy
was usually an expensive form of government and could be
maintained only by heavy taxation, so heavy in some states
that the propertied class regarded it as little short of confiscation. It is not surprising, therefore, that in most Greek democracies there was an oligarchic party, or that this party was
often ready to resort to almost any means to escape the burdens
imposed by the existing government. To many of these parties
the independence of their city state must have seemed a matter
of small moment as compared with the immediate relief which
would follow an oligarchic revolution, and their dominant
rivals must have feared such a revolution for the same reason.
It is unlikely that they put their motives either to themselves
or to others in purely economic terms, and sentiment no doubt
played a real part in their contests; but sentiment never acts so
powerfully as when it has behind it strong material interests.
The degree of animosity which the two parties felt for each
other must have varied greatly from one state to another and

at different periods in the same state, and probably in some it never became very intense; but it was sufficiently widespread and general to be a striking characteristic of the Greek city states. Even in Athens the conflict was present beneath the surface, as the events of the Peloponnesian War showed clearly, although her situation was peculiarly favorable in that she was able to meet part of the cost of assisting her poorer citizens by taxing her allies. Nevertheless the wealthy Athenians did not escape lightly, and many of them secretly resented what they regarded as the excesses of the democracy, and as soon as there seemed the least chance of success were ready to join in an attempt to set up some form of oligarchy.

To view the oligarchic party simply as the propertied class and the democrats as the poor is doubtless to simplify the situation unduly, for economic interests are always more complex than such broad generalizations allow for. It is easy to imagine wholly probable circumstances in which both classes would be more or less divided between the two parties; for example, the interests of the landowners might be in such sharp conflict with those of the trading and industrial class that the merchants and manufacturers would prefer the burdens of democracy to the rule of an agricultural oligarchy. Such a condition might easily arise in some of the subject allies of Athens, because an oligarchic revolution would in some cases result in the immediate closing of their principal markets. Nor is it necessary to suppose that the interests of the landowners were so similar that they were always a united group, since those who sold their crops to merchants for export would have a more or less strong motive for taking the same side. We are, therefore, justified in assuming that in many states of the Empire the line of cleavage between democrats and oligarchs cut through all classes, that the parties were of a somewhat mixed character, and that neither was entirely united in its aims and convictions. In fact democracy and oligarchy are not fixed and definite things like chemical elements, but each admits of many varieties and modifications. The revolution of 411 B.C. which set up the Council of Four Hundred at Athens brought to light wide differences in the oligarchic party as to what kind of oligarchy they wanted, and similar differences no doubt existed in the other states.

When all qualifications are made, however, it remains true that the two parties existed in most, probably in all, the states of the Athenian Empire, and that Athens, as the champion and protector of democracy, secured the more or less loyal support of the democrats. Of course her policy made enemies of the oligarchs, but it may have been the wisest which she could have pursued. The events of the Peloponnesian War revealed the sentiments of the allies after some fifty years of Athenian imperialism. The revolts that then occurred were all the work of the oligarchs, and the masses only permitted them, or joined in them, reluctantly and under strong pressure of some kind. It seems evident from their conduct that the democrats felt little, if any, resentment toward Athens and that they were, upon the whole, satisfied to remain under her rule. To picture the subject states of the Empire as seething with discontent and eager to take advantage of the first opportunity to throw off the yoke, as is sometimes done, is to misunderstand the whole situation. Such a picture is probably true of the oligarchic parties, but they were after all a small, though active and powerful, minority, whose sentiments were not shared by the majority of the people. In spite of the defects of the Athenian Empire, and they were probably much more numerous than we have any means of knowing, and in spite of her systematic exploitation of her subjects for her own profit, the supremacy of Athens did not rest wholly on the power of her fleet or the fear of her vengeance. In addition to these the Empire had so broad a base of popular support that it could not be seriously shaken until the power of Athens seemed hopelessly broken by the Sicilian disaster.

PART II

ROME

I

AGRICULTURAL DEPRESSION AND THE ARMY

The causes of the fall of the Roman Republic have been little discussed by historians, perhaps because they have generally felt that these causes were made sufficiently plain by the mere narrative of events. Certainly they have seldom tried to get below the surface and have usually been content with a few general statements. Of such generalities the most common is that a city state could not govern an empire and that the Roman Republic, being a city state, fell when it attempted the impossible task. Other causes commonly implied, when not explicitly stated, are the gradual corruption of the nobles, the people, and the army, and the consequent misgovernment of the provinces. An examination of these reasons at once reveals their unsatisfactory character, for they have the rather serious defect of being based on false assumptions. It is simply not true that a city state could not govern an empire: Rome actually did so for one hundred and fifty years, and in view of that fact it seems necessary to go further and seek to determine why she finally ceased to be able to do it. The corruption of all classes is generally taken as leading to the breaking down of the government at home and to the oppression and pillaging of the provinces. As to the last point, anyone who reads the story can see at once that the provinces, however badly they were governed, had nothing to do directly with the overthrow of the Republic. It was Roman armies and not rebellious provincials that established the Empire, and, if Rome's subjects profited by the new form of government, they took no part in setting it up. As to the corruption within the Roman state, it has no essential bearing on the problem because the Republic did not cease to work, however badly, until it was definitely stopped by the intervention of armed force. Undoubtedly there is some truth in the causes mentioned, but, when given in such general terms, they manifestly fail as explanations.

In the light of recent experience it should be possible to look at the fall of the Roman Republic from a somewhat new point of view. The establishment of a dictatorship on the ruins of a constitutional government no longer presents itself as a phenomenon peculiar to ancient times and we have now no excuse for imagining that it can be adequately explained by vague phrases about the lack of representative institutions and the inability of a city state to govern an empire. We have seen that national governments fully equipped with representative institutions are no more safe from dictatorship than were the ancient city states. Today we might, perhaps, give the general cause of dictatorships as the breakdown, real or apparent, of constitutional government when confronted by problems of such urgency as to require immediate action. Such a generalization is, of course, much too general to be of value unless accompanied by a bill of particulars. In each instance we need to examine carefully the nature of the problems which demanded solution and the reasons why no solution could be found by constitutional methods. Such an investigation in the case of the Roman Republic is the purpose of the following pages. In this chapter a brief study will be made of the problem which was immediately fatal to the Republic, in the next an attempt will be made to determine why the Republic was unable to solve this problem, and in the third the circumstances under which the Republic perished will be examined.

Since the army took the leading part in the overthrow of the Republic, it is obvious that the problem was a military one. It is also obvious that the army did not become dangerous to constitutional government until the growth of the empire forced the Republic to abandon its original military system and to reorganize its army. This reorganization was brought about by Marius, but he had hardly carried it through before the state discovered that it was totally unable to control the new army. Here then are two questions to which some sort of answer must be found: why did the old military system break down, and why was the new army unmanageable?

Like many of the peoples of ancient times, the Romans at first regarded military service as a duty which went with the possession of property, since it was only those citizens who were possessed of some means who could be expected or required to provide themselves with the necessary equipment in the shape of arms and armor. Moreover, in early Italy the chief form of property was land, and the army was, therefore, made up of the landowners. Until the time of Marius the Roman army continued to be recruited on this theory, and the soldiers who conquered Italy, broke Carthage, and established Rome's supremacy over the Mediterranean world were in the main small farmers. In early days they had served more or less willingly, because the wars of Rome were wars to protect their farms and a defeat might mean that their property would be pillaged or destroyed. After Rome had conquered the peoples in her immediate vicinity, however, this became less and less true, so that, as the wars were fought farther and farther away, some degree of compulsion became necessary. The state accordingly developed a regular system of conscription by which every landowner was liable for service in the legions, and the required number each year was selected by some form of draft. When the campaign was over, the farmer was discharged and went back to his farm, for the Romans made no attempt to organize a regular standing army, but raised such forces as were needed at the moment and disbanded them as soon as the need was over. In the course of time the state found itself obliged to do more and more for the men, to feed them, to provide some part of their equipment, to pay them for their lost time. Nevertheless, the army retained much of its original character; it was still an army of small farmers conscripted into the legions and chiefly anxious to get back home again. It was, then, with a conscript army of small farmers that Rome established her empire, but the military needs of that empire ultimately made this kind of army inadequate.

When Rome acquired provinces outside Italy, she found it necessary to maintain permanent garrisons in them in order to keep the peace and protect the frontiers. As the number of provinces increased, they called for larger and larger forces, so that the demands of the state for men grew steadily greater. In early days Rome did not usually put in the field more than four legions at once, but after 200 B.C. the number was seldom less than eight and frequently rose to ten or twelve. Unless the number of the small farmers increased in proportion, it was bound to become more and more difficult to find the men. Not only were more men required, but the service became more and more burdensome in other ways. When conscripts were sent across the sea to serve in distant provinces, it was impossible to discharge them as promptly as in the past. The term of service, therefore, was inevitably lengthened and the farmer was kept from his farm for a longer period, often with serious consequences to him. It was possible for him to serve for a few months, or even a year, without too great a loss, but when Rome annexed Spain (201 B.C.), it was found necessary to keep the recruits in the legions there for six years, and doubtless they were kept for two or three years in the other provinces. When at length the soldier did return to his farm, in many cases he found that his family had been unable to keep it up in his absence; often it was seriously run down, often no doubt mortgaged, sometimes lost altogether. He brought with him on his return whatever he had saved from his pay and whatever share he had received of the booty won by the army. Such resources must frequently have been very inadequate, since the Roman armies met with many defeats and defeat yielded no booty. Often the small farmer must have been ruined by his service in the legions, so that we can hardly wonder that he was less and less anxious to serve, or that the conscription became more and more unpopular. In fact the growth of the empire was putting an intolerable burden on the small farmers of Italy, and this was only made worse by certain other changes which were taking place as a direct result of Roman expansion.

When Rome annexed Sicily in 241 B.C. at the close of the First Punic War, she collected from the provincials the same tribute which they had been accustomed to pay to their former rulers. This tribute consisted of one-tenth of the crop, and, since the Roman state had no machinery for collecting it, her statesmen adopted the simple expedient of farming the tax. By this system the right to collect the tithe in the different districts was sold to the individual or group of individuals who would agree to pay the state the highest sum for the privilege. Having obtained the contract, the tax farmers sent their agents through the district and collected their tenth. The principal crop of the island was grain, and the contracts usually called not for a money payment but for the delivery of a certain amount of grain to the Roman government. What remained above this amount the tax farmers had to dispose of as best they could. The price of grain being higher in Italy than in Sicily and water transportation being cheap, the simplest way to dispose of the grain was to ship it to Rome or some of the other cities on the coast of the peninsula. Since the tax farmer had paid nothing for the grain except the cost of collection, it could be sold at a very low price and still yield a profit. Moreover, the Roman government used the grain which it received to feed the army, but very often a considerable surplus remained at the end of the year, and this was thrown on the market and sold for whatever it would bring.

The annexation of Sicily thus resulted in a sharp fall in the price of grain in many parts of Italy, and the consequences to the small farmer were disastrous. The large landowner was much less seriously affected, because, having command of capital, he could meet the situation by turning his attention to other crops. He could, for example, set out olive orchards or vineyards, but such a remedy was impossible to the small farmer because after a vineyard was planted it took some time for it to mature and during part of this time the land could not be put to any other profitable use. Without capital the small farmer must perforce go on raising what he could. In many places the influx of the cheap grain from Sicily meant ruin, and the small farmers abandoned, lost, or sold their farms and drifted to the cities, especially Rome, to pick up a precarious livelihood as members of the city rabble. Once they left the country and ceased to own land, they were no longer liable for service in the army, so that the burden became all the heavier on such as still contrived to get a living on their farms. In estimating the effects of the cheap grain we must bear in mind that it only reached certain parts of Italy, namely those to which it could be easily and cheaply transported.

This meant in fact the southern and western coasts; the grain could not penetrate far into the interior, because land transportation was expensive. A large part of Italy was probably not affected at all, and in some regions the effect must have been slight, or at any rate not ruinous.[1] Still the disturbance which the cheap grain created was sufficiently widespread and serious to have important consequences, for it wiped out the small farmers in many districts at a time when the government's demands for men were rapidly increasing. The Italian peasantry could have continued to meet these demands if they had been a rapidly increasing class, but as it was, their number grew very slowly for a time and then began actually to decrease.

While this was happening in Italy, the Roman empire abroad was steadily expanding and with each new province more men were required for the legions even in time of peace. It was not that the Roman government was deliberately imperialistic or that it delighted in conquest and annexation; in point of fact it strove earnestly to avoid both. It had taken the first steps in the acquisition of an empire chiefly as a measure of defense to safeguard Italy itself. Once a beginning had been made, however, it proved impossible to stop: entangled in the meshes of foreign alliances, Rome was reluctantly obliged to extend her power and her responsibilities farther and farther afield. Since the growth of the empire could not be arrested, it was only a question of time when the small farmers in Italy would no longer be able to supply the soldiers necessary to protect and maintain it. Sooner or later Rome would be forced

---

[1] Probably the effect was most serious and widespread in the south, where the country had been widely devastated during the Second Punic War. This devastation must have ruined many of the small farmers and plunged most of those who returned to their farms so heavily in debt that even a small decrease in the price of grain was fatal.

to reconstruct her military system and to find a substitute for the small farmer.

The difficulty of getting enough recruits was becoming so great that desperate attempts were made to increase the number of small farmers. This was the main purpose which Tiberius Gracchus had in view in his agrarian legislation (133 B.C.), if we may trust the accounts which have come down to us of the arguments by which he justified it. What he did was in substance to divide the public land among the poor in small holdings, first taking this land away from the rich who had managed to get possession of most of it. In this way the reformer broke up many large estates, ruined many wealthy though otherwise innocent people, stirred up bitter political strife, and got himself murdered by a mob of rich and furious gentlemen, but he did nevertheless succeed in creating a considerable number of small farmers. What he achieved, however, was quite insufficient to save the old military system, and as soon as the demands of the state became exceptionally heavy, a new recruiting ground for the army had to be discovered and exploited.

The change began in 108 B.C., and in the seven years which followed Marius reconstructed the military system. He was elected consul for 107 to put an end to a war in which Rome had become involved with a north African king named Jugurtha. The first task of Marius was to recruit soldiers to reinforce the army in Africa, and, as a result of long experience, he was well aware that the conscription was extremely unpopular and that the reluctant farmers whom it forced into the legions made very poor soldiers. He solved the difficulty by discarding the conscription and calling for volunteers and easily succeeded in getting as many soldiers as he wanted. The call and the response to it marked an epoch in the history of the Republic. The old army was dead and henceforth the wars of Rome were fought with volunteer armies.[2] Probably few at the time realized the significance of the change, but it soon became so clear that none could shut their eyes to it. An army was now raised by a new method. The state appointed a general to conduct a war, who then called for volunteers, but he could get them only if there was confidence in his success, that is, only if he had somehow acquired a reputation as a soldier. Now the number of men at any given time who had been able to gain such a reputation was very limited, and the state was obliged to choose its generals from this small circle whenever it needed an army at a crisis. Once the general was invested with the command, it was possible to remove him and appoint another in his place only under exceptional circumstances, for the men who had taken service under a general because of their confidence in *him* would not usually be willing to accept anyone else. The army recruited by the general was *his* army rather than the army of the state. How close the ties were that bound the soldiers to their commander we can only hope to appreciate when we have seen who the volunteers were and why they were willing to enlist.

It has long been a commonplace that the volunteer armies of the later Republic were proletarian in character, but few historians have troubled to examine the matter more closely. There were then in Italy two very distinct classes to whom the term may be applied. In Rome, and probably in the other cities of the peninsula, there was the urban rabble, living from hand to mouth and depending to a large degree on the bounty of the state, which in Rome was supplied by the corn law.

---

[2]Conscription was never formally abolished, and it was, no doubt, occasionally resorted to after this time, but the course of events seems to show that it was not used extensively enough to affect the general character of the armies.

This is what historians have usually understood by the proletariat, but it seems fairly certain that the urban rabble contributed comparatively little to the volunteer armies. At any
rate, all the available evidence seems to point in a different
direction, and to indicate that the soldiers of the later Republic
came chiefly from the country districts. The favorite recruiting ground of Pompey was apparently Picenum, and at the outbreak of the Civil War we find him levying troops in all parts
of Italy except Rome, of which there is no mention, while
Caesar raised most of his legions in Cisalpine Gaul. In this
connection Pompey's plans after his return from the East in
62 B.C. are highly suggestive; to reward his disbanded soldiers
a large sum of money was to be accumulated in the treasury
with which land was to be purchased and allotted to the men.
If the majority of his army had been drawn from the city, it
is rather difficult to see why land should have been demanded
instead of a cash bonus, but, if the dominant element came
from the country, the preference for land is easily understood. We may conclude, therefore, with some confidence that
the new armies, like the old, were mainly recruited in the rural
districts and from the classes engaged in agriculture. The real
change which resulted from the new system was that the landowner dropped out of the legions and his place was taken by
volunteers belonging to that section of the rural population
who did not own land; the small farmer remained at home
on his farm and the man who went to the wars was a member
of the rural proletariat.

That such a proletariat existed is easy enough to prove.
Large estates were, indeed, common in Italy, but, while they
were cultivated mainly by slave labor, they gave employment
to a great many free laborers as well, particularly at certain
seasons of the year. It is obvious that if the owner of a vineyard bought enough slaves to handle the vintage some of them

would have very little to do during most of the year. It was more profitable to have a smaller number of slaves and to hire free laborers for the vintage, and the same thing would be true of all kinds of large estates. That these considerations were fully understood we have definite evidence in the two works on agriculture which have come down to us from Roman times. Both Cato and Varro make it clear that in spite of slavery there was room for many free laborers in rural Italy. Such free laborers may have formed the bulk of the rural proletariat, but many of them must have had some other source of livelihood, since their employment on the large estates would be seasonal in character. There was probably no hard and fast line between these farm hands and several other classes which must have been more or less numerous in the country, such as tenant farmers, peasant proprietors whose holdings were too small to support their owners, sons of farmers anxious to increase the family income or their own. No doubt we should include also some of the poorer townsfolk, who could quit their jobs for a time or who had no jobs to quit but who were willing to work when work was to be found. Altogether there must have been in the country districts a very numerous class, living wholly or partly by agriculture, with very little prospect of any improvement in their condition. The cherished ambition of such men would naturally be to acquire a farm of their own, free from debt and large enough to support them in what they regarded as comfort. After the military reforms of Marius this class saw in the army the shortest and most direct, if not the only possible, way to reach their goal, and it seems to have been from the rural proletariat that most of the volunteers came. They enlisted in the hope that after a few years of military service they would be able to return to the land and establish themselves as substantial and prosperous farmers, and the general under whom they believed that such hopes would be realized was the only one who could readily find soldiers to fill his legions.

The volunteer, then, enlisted in order to secure a farm, and it is necessary to consider carefully how he expected to get it. A soldier when he received his discharge would, of course, have whatever part of his pay he had contrived to save, but this would hardly be enough for him to count upon it seriously. Much more important under fortunate circumstances was his share of the booty. In ancient times the conditions of war were very different from those which prevail today; the pillage of the enemy was sanctioned, and prisoners taken in battle might be, and very often were, sold as slaves. The general and the state received a portion of the spoils, but a part went to the soldiers. How much or how little they would get was a very uncertain matter and depended to a considerable extent upon the general. He might allow his troops to loot a captured town at his discretion, and he might distribute some of the prisoners among them to be sold for their own profit. The attitude of the general, therefore, had a good deal to do with what his soldiers obtained in the way of spoils and his success in the field had even more. To loot towns they must first be captured, and to sell prisoners they must first be taken. If the general were defeated, it was clear that there would be no booty, and disaster in the field might cost the soldiers their lives or their freedom. The first thing to consider, therefore, when enlisting under any general was whether he was likely to win, and the second, whether if successful he was likely to deal generously with his men. To get an army he must have such a reputation that the rural proletariat felt certain of both victory and reward under him. If he met their expectations, the volunteers might hope that when the war was over and the army disbanded they would bring home a considerable sum out of their pay and their share of the booty. But, after all, they

could hardly expect that this sum would be sufficient to purchase the coveted farm in the open market. Few campaigns
could supply plunder on such a scale, and generals in search
of recruits soon found it necessary to offer a further induce-
ment by promising to secure for their men a bonus from the
state in the form of an allotment of land. Such promises were
easy enough to make, but they were frequently very hard to
fulfil, and the rural proletariat was quite aware of this. Before
they enlisted, they would have to have some assurance that the
general was likely to be both able and willing to make good his
word. It will be clear, then, that to raise an army under the
volunteer system required a general who had somehow managed to secure the confidence of the Italian peasantry in a very
high degree. They must believe in his military skill, in his
liberal treatment of his men, in his loyalty to his word, and in
his power as well as his inclination to keep it. His obligations
to his men were at once military and political: while the war
lasted, his obvious duty was to win it; once it was over he
became forthwith a politician who must somehow contrive to
secure the promised land for his veterans. A general could no
longer lay down his arms and retire into private life after he
had won a victory; the character of his army and the means
by which he had raised it forced him to take an active part
in politics until he had redeemed his pledges. How these
pledges could or should be redeemed was often a very serious
problem.

The promise which the general held out of a bonus in land
was a purely personal one on his part, the state having assumed
no responsibility whatever. It meant simply that he would
use his power and influence to the utmost to induce the government to provide the necessary land, and it was accepted by the
volunteers because they believed that his power and influence
would be sufficient. How then was the state to find the land

to make good the general's promises? In early times the state
had had a very large amount of public land in Italy, but most
of this had been disposed of by the time of Marius. The land
was now practically all held by private owners, and to provide for an army was, therefore, a difficult matter. There were
in fact only two ways in which the land could be obtained,
namely, confiscation and purchase. At the beginning it seems
to have been chiefly the first of these which was employed, but
it was used outside Italy. The wars in which the soldiers had
been engaged furnished pretexts for confiscating considerable
amounts of land which could be distributed among the men
without serious opposition. The objection to this simple solution was that it obliged the veterans to settle in the provinces.
While there were some provinces in which they were not unwilling to live, there were others to which they were much less
attracted, so that ultimately the state was faced by demands
for land in Italy itself, demands which could only be met by
measures certain to arouse bitter opposition. A brief examination of the manner in which the more important of the volunteer armies were disposed of will serve, perhaps, to make the
issue involved clearer and more definite.

The first army of the new type was raised by Marius for the
war against Jugurtha, whose kingdom of Numidia was situated
in what is now known as Algeria. At some time after the war a
number of the veterans were settled in Africa, and it is probable
that the rest were disposed of along with the next army.
Marius had hardly finished with Jugurtha, when he was
recalled to Italy with his troops to protect the peninsula from
the threatened invasion of the Cimbri and Teutones. These
wandering German tribes postponed their attack for some time,
and Marius recruited additional men and finally defeated them
in 101 B.C. To dispose of the soldiers Marius had a bill passed
by one of the tribunes which provided for the allotment of land

in southern France, or, as the Romans called it, Transalpine Gaul, and for the planting of a number of colonies in the other provinces. The bill encountered much opposition, the causes of which will be discussed later, and was carried by violence, so that it was afterwards declared null and void, but under it Marius seems to have established at least one colony in Corsica and perhaps others elsewhere of which no evidence has come down to us. It is also possible that some of the land in Gaul was actually assigned to the soldiers, but here again definite evidence is lacking. However much or little the disbanded soldiers really got, the method adopted for dealing with them is clear: they were to be sent off to the provinces, where land could be found for them without disturbing anybody but provincials, who did not count, and the provinces involved seem to have been those where the soldiers were not unwilling to settle.

The next important volunteer army which had to be disposed of was that with which Sulla defeated Mithridates of Pontus, an ambitious and energetic king in Asia Minor (84 B.C.). Rome was now in the throes of bitter party struggles, in which Sulla supported the senatorial faction. While he was in the East, the other side got the upper hand in Rome, deposed him from his command, and declared him an outlaw. To the fulminations of the democratic government in Rome Sulla paid not the slightest attention, and, what was more to the point, his soldiers stood firmly by him, for he was a commander after their own heart, in whose ability and liberality they had entire confidence. When he had defeated Mithridates and forced him to make peace, Sulla returned to Italy at the head of his army (83 B.C.). Between him and the men in power in Rome there could be no truce and a brief but bloody civil war followed, in which Sulla beat down all resistance and made himself absolute

master of Italy. This civil war greatly simplified the problem of disposing of his victorious army, and by relentlessly
proscribing his opponents and confiscating their property he
secured the land with which to provide for his veterans.

With Sulla's death (78 B.C.) the star of Pompey rose rapidly. He had been one of Sulla's lieutenants in the civil war
and had managed to acquire a wide popularity and a high
military reputation in certain regions of Italy, a reputation
which was perhaps considerably higher than he really deserved.
The government, which the death of Sulla left in a somewhat
precarious position, soon found itself obliged to make use of
his services to put down a revolt of those whose land Sulla had
confiscated, and then sent him to Spain to deal with a formidable insurrection which had broken out in that country. He
had hardly restored order there when he was hastily summoned
to return to Italy with his army to assist in putting down an
uprising of slaves and gladiators which the general in charge,
Crassus, seemed unable to crush. Pompey returned, but
Crassus put an end to the danger before he arrived (71 B.C.).
Nevertheless, he was able and willing to profit by the situation.
He decided that he wished to be consul and agreed to take
Crassus as his colleague to avoid the necessity of a civil war.
Neither was legally eligible, but their armies were unanswer-
able arguments and they were duly elected consuls for 70
B.C. What they did with their armies we have no definite
information, but they managed somehow to get rid of them.
We may conjecture that the soldiers of Crassus were not the
usual type of volunteers, for they had been recruited to fight
the rebel slaves, and probably in such a cause the small farmers
were ready and willing to enlist, since their own property was
in danger. It is not unlikely that many, perhaps most, of them
asked nothing better than to be disbanded and allowed to go
home once more. It is possible, at least, that many of Pompey's

men were provided for in Spain, where plenty of land could be found for the purpose. At any rate, the armies were disbanded and vanished forthwith from history, and Rome enjoyed a lull of three or four years.

It then became necessary to give Pompey a new command. For some years Rome had been engaged in another war with Mithridates, which was now going so badly for the Romans that Pompey was put in charge (66 B.C.). He accomplished his mission successfully and disbanded his army on his return to Italy in 62. Although disbanded, his veterans were not provided for, and Pompey set himself to secure for them the coveted land. The methods hitherto used to reward an army could not be resorted to in this case, for the war had been fought in the interior of Asia Minor, where the soldiers had no desire to settle, and they were demanding land in Italy itself. This demand presented difficulties, but Pompey devised a plan which was, perhaps, as good as the circumstances admitted. He found himself, however, involved in politics and was unable to accomplish anything until in desperation he was induced to join the coalition known in history as the First Triumvirate (60 B.C.), with which the Republic may be said to have come to an end.

But although the new armies were dangerous to the state, it was impossible to do without them. The old system had broken down so completely that no one could seriously propose to revive it. To have attempted to conscript the small farmers when volunteers were easily to be found by the right general would certainly have provoked a storm. Moreover, the last armies raised by the old method were obviously inefficient and manageable only with difficulty. The recruits seem to have been drafted for a comparatively short term of service, so that every year some of the men were replaced by fresh levies, consisting of raw recruits anxious to get home as soon as possible, a sentiment which was fully shared by the rest of the army. Under such conditions it was no easy matter to maintain discipline, and the best trained men were constantly leaving. The troubles in the army of which we hear so much in the war against Jugurtha cannot have been due entirely to the incompetence of the generals, but must have been partly the natural result of the character of the army. As a fighting machine there can be no doubt that the new type of army was a great improvement on the old. The men now enlisted for the duration of the war rather than for any fixed term. In theory there may, or may not, have been a definite period for which the volunteer agreed to serve, but in practice this was entirely unimportant. The soldier had enlisted in the hope of getting a farm and he could not expect his general to take much trouble to reward men who left him before the war was ended and victory achieved. The army which began a campaign thus acquired a permanent character, and it was comparatively easy to maintain discipline, for the soldiers who hoped so much from their general could not afford to challenge his authority or incur his displeasure. Moreover, strict discipline and rigorous training were obviously to the advantage of the soldiers, since the higher the efficiency of the army the sooner the fighting would be over and the promised rewards could be enjoyed. Thus the army had as strong an interest in success as the general and would work strenuously for its attainment.

The volunteer armies have often been called "professional" armies by historians, but this expression is a very misleading one. No doubt there were professional soldiers among the Romans, but they were likely to be found chiefly among the legions who did garrison duty in the provinces in time of peace. These troops, who formed what may be called the standing army of the Republic, must be sharply distinguished from the special armies which were raised from time to time for particular wars. The standing army may have had a more or less professional character and the men doubtless enlisted for a regular term of service, but the special army recruited for a special campaign had a different character altogether. The volunteer who enlisted in one of these knew that he would have to fight for the duration of the war, and he could confidently trust the state to relieve the treasury of unnecessary expense by discharging him as soon as the war was over. In no sense, therefore, did he take up arms as a profession, but only as a means to becoming a prosperous farmer as soon as possible.

In conclusion it may be well to sum up briefly the nature of the Roman military system and the problem which this system presented to the government. It should be borne in mind that the Republic never attempted to maintain a large standing army in time of peace. The ordinary forces of the state were barely sufficient to keep order in the provinces and protect their frontiers against border raids, and were seldom adequate to guard against any serious attack, never indeed unless the attack was anticipated. In case war broke out, or an emergency of any sort arose, the government raised a special army which was disbanded when it had accomplished its purpose. How the ordinary forces of the state were raised we have little information; probably the recruits were volunteers, as was the case with the special armies. Neither do we know the size of the regular army, which doubtless varied from year to year according to what were supposed to be the requirements of the moment. On the average perhaps ten to twelve legions would be a fair estimate, and this would mean a force of about 50,000 to 60,000 men, for the legions seem seldom to have been at their full strength. It was probably possible to find some 10,000 volunteers a year who were ready to enlist merely for the pay and their share of any booty which might be taken in fighting against bandits and repelling raids on the frontier. Those who joined the regular army could expect no bonus in land, since they were sent out, discharged, and sent home in small groups, the volunteers for each year being distributed among the provinces to replace the soldiers whose term of enlistment had expired. The inadequacy of the regular army for its task of frontier defense was probably due, in part at least, to the limited number of recruits who were attracted by the conditions of ordinary provincial service.

Since the standing army was barely large enough for times of comparative tranquility, when the Republic was forced to engage in a serious war, a special army had to be raised. When such an army became necessary, the government appointed a general to take charge of the war, and this general gathered his recruits and organized them. To secure volunteers he promised, either explicitly or implicitly, that he would secure land for them when the war was over. Once such an army had been raised it was practically irresistible. Pompey during his war with Mithridates (66–63 B.C.) seems to have had under his command about 40,000 men. While he remained at the head of this army, the state was obviously at his mercy, for he had almost as large a force as the entire regular army, and that regular army was widely scattered and divided among a number of different commanders, many of whom had no military reputation. This last point is important, because the common soldiers were not likely to support leaders in whom they had little confidence against the great Pompey, whose name was a synonym for victory. The Republic could not, therefore, look to its ordinary troops for the slightest help against him, and it could resist him only by commissioning another general to raise another special army to fight him. This was only possible if there was at hand someone with a military reputation at least comparable to that of Pompey, and, if this expedient were resorted to and succeeded, then the state would be at the mercy of the new general as completely as it had been at Pompey's. There was, therefore, no way of escape; until the commander of a special army had disbanded it, the government had no choice but to ratify his will if he chose to assert it so categorically that evasion or delay was impossible. Yet the state had at first a certain negative force as the embodiment of the law, for which both soldiers and generals had some respect. If this respect was sufficient to induce the general to disband his army before his demands had been complied with, as Pompey did in 62 B.C., the veterans still constituted a serious problem for the state, and the general must continue to take an active part in public life until his men had received their reward.

It is obvious that such special armies were a danger to the Republic because the government had no real control over them. They belonged not to the state but to their general, and a government which has no serious hold on the allegiance of its army is evidently in a very precarious situation and can hardly hope to endure for any great length of time. If the danger was obvious, the remedy was equally so. The cause of the state's weakness was that the soldiers looked to their general to find some means of providing them with the land for which they had enlisted in the legions. The remedy was for the government itself to undertake to provide the land. If the soldiers could be persuaded to trust the state, the chief tie which bound them to their commander would be broken. Why, then, we may reasonably ask, did not the Roman government attempt to do something of the kind? The answer would seem to be that it could not. To provide for the soldiers would have required a definite and settled policy, but by the time that such provision had become necessary the government of the Republic had become so disorganized as to be incapable of any settled policy; in other words, the political instability had become so great that a solution of the military problem was practically impossible.   To understand this it will be necessary to examine briefly how the Republic was actually governed in the days of its greatness and why the conquest of the Mediterranean world gradually destroyed its efficiency.

II

MACHINE POLITICS AND EFFICIENCY

It is a striking proof of the political capacity of the Romans that they were able to work successfully a constitution so abundantly provided with checks and balances as to make efficient government almost impossible. The executive and judicial functions were entrusted to two consuls and several praetors, eight in the last days of the Republic. The consuls were the highest magistrates, and each had a veto on every act of the other; unless they happened to be in agreement, therefore, neither could do anything. Moreover, they were changed every year, immediate re-election being forbidden by law, so that the state could not look to them for anything in the nature of a continuous policy. Even when the consuls were in harmony, they might find themselves powerless to act because of the opposition of the tribunes. There were ten tribunes, each of whom could veto any act of any magistrate, including his nine colleagues and the two consuls. Any one of the ten tribunes could thus put a stop to any governmental action in Rome, but fortunately they could not leave the city and hence could not interfere with the generals at the head of the armies. In the capital, however, nothing could be done if a single tribune chose to use his veto. Of course matters were not quite so bad in practice as they seem in theory. No government would work without continual compromises, and the Romans made them just as other peoples do; even so, it is clear that the opportunities for obstruction which the Roman constitution provided were exceptionally numerous. Aside altogether from the possibility of obstruction, it is obvious that a double-headed executive changing every year was incapable of giving the state a steady and settled policy.

The necessary continuity in the government was contributed by the senate. This body was composed of the ex-magistrates and numbered about 300 members at first, but about 600 after the time of Sulla. Since the senators held their seats for life, the composition of the senate changed very slowly. In constitutional theory its function was almost purely advisory; it met only when summoned by one of the magistrates, it could vote only on motions put to it by some magistrate, and its decrees when passed were not legally binding on the magistrates. In spite of its theoretical weakness, however, the senate found means to exert a very real control and to direct the policy of the state.

The supreme authority was by the Roman constitution lodged in the popular assembly, which was a mass meeting which every Roman citizen could attend. In theory the assembly was the Roman people, but in practice it was that fraction of the people, large or small, which happened to be present on any given occasion. Those who were there acted in the name of the whole and the absent were ignored, just as today we ignore those citizens who do not take the trouble to vote. There is, however, an important difference to be noted: under our modern system nearly all the citizens *can* vote if they choose to do so, but in Rome many of them lived so far from the city that it was practically impossible for them to attend the assembly. To this fact the Romans paid no attention, and no attempt was made to devise any system of representation. The assembly elected all magistrates, and thus indirectly the senators, and made the laws. In legislation the people possessed

no initiative and could simply accept or reject a bill submitted
to them by a magistrate. Laws could be proposed by the consuls, praetors, and tribunes, but one tribune could veto a bill
and so prevent its enactment even though it was supported by
the other nine tribunes as well as by both consuls and all the
praetors. If it was able to act, the assembly was absolutely
supreme, for it was impossible to declare a law unconstitutional.
If it conflicted with the constitution, it merely amended the
constitution in that particular; in other words, there was no
distinction between an ordinary statute and a constitutional
amendment, and any legal enactment of the assembly was final
and binding. In theory the senate had only one power over
legislation: it could determine whether all the proper formali-
ties had been observed in the enactment of a law, and, if they
had not, it could declare the law null and void on the ground
that it had never been legally passed. If this happened, the
assembly could, if it chose, pass the law again, taking care to
observe the required forms. The people could in theory enact
any laws they pleased, for the fact that bills must be brought
before the assembly by a magistrate was no real limitation
on their power, since, if they wished to pass a law, they had
only to elect magistrates who would introduce the measure
they desired. In theory again the assembly could interfere
with the conduct of the government to any extent it pleased,
since it could pass a law requiring the magistrates to pursue a
certain policy or to do a certain definite and specific thing, but
in fact the people left the direction of affairs very largely in
the hands of the senate.

In the Roman government there was thus a wide gulf between theory and practice. In the strict constitutional sense
the senate had no control over legislation or over the action
of the magistrates. It could advise the magistrates to adopt a

certain policy or not to bring a certain bill before the people, but the magistrates were free to follow its advice or not at their discretion. In fact, however, the senate was able for a very long period to get its advice followed and its decisions accepted without serious question, so that it was to all intents and purposes the governing body of the Republic. How are we to explain the undoubted fact of its long and almost absolute supremacy? The explanations usually offered by historians seem somewhat superficial. A few obvious points have been noticed, a few cool assumptions made without any particular evidence in their support, and the problem has been dismissed as solved. Since there is something in these explanations, it may be well to review them briefly. In dealing with the magistrates the fact that the senate was composed of ex-magistrates who held their seats for life undoubtedly gave it an advantage. A man was not eligible for the higher magistracies until he had held some of the lower ones, and, since these lower offices conferred a seat in the senate, the praetors and consuls, as well as most of the tribunes, were senators before their election to these offices and would continue to be senators for the rest of their lives after their terms expired. Most of them, therefore, would prefer to exalt the senate, of which they were permanent members, rather than the offices which they held for so short a time. But does this take us far? If the senate were divided into parties, would not this division be reflected in the conduct of the magistrates? Why should a consul who belonged to the minority party accept and follow the advice of the majority? In fact, when such a situation arose, there was trouble, but the situation rarely did arise because the senate was *not* divided into parties, although of course there were often differences of opinion among the senators. In spite of such differences, however, the senate managed to maintain so surprising a degree of unity over so long a period that we must look further for some explanation of it.

As against the assembly the senate was able to maintain its supremacy simply because for a long time its authority was not seriously challenged. Why, then, did the Roman people acquiesce in the senate's control of affairs for over one hundred and fifty years? To explain this, historians have pointed to the success of the senate's government and have assumed that the people realized its superior competence. The masses, we are told, were awed by the firmness, wisdom, and patriotism of the conscript fathers and refrained from interfering in matters which they did not understand. If we look into the facts a little, we shall find ample reason to think that the senate committed many grave blunders in its policy and that its government often gave rather ghastly exhibitions of incompetence. The Roman people certainly had frequent excuse for feeling that they could manage things as well as the senate was doing, but they left the senate to correct its own mistakes and to find a way out of the difficulties in which it had involved the state. Such patience calls for explanation and the one offered seems somewhat inadequate.

There is, however, another and more satisfactory explanation, so obvious that it could not escape notice, namely, that the Roman government was not in the least what it was supposed to be. In theory it was something like a democracy, but it never was one in practice. Although every Roman citizen was eligible to the highest offices of the state, in fact these offices were passed around among the members of a small governing class. This class was known as the nobility, and the government of the senate was only another name for the government of the nobles. Since the nobles contrived to secure an almost complete monopoly of the offices, it followed that they automatically filled the senate, which was merely a sort of caucus of the nobility. In it the members of the governing class got together, discussed public affairs, and decided on the policy which should be pursued. These decisions were accepted for the simple reason that it was the governing class which made them.

Since for over one hundred and fifty years the nobles dominated the Republic, it will be desirable to see who they were and what they were like. The Romans applied the term noble (*nobilis*) to any man whose ancestors had held one of the higher offices. The first member of a family to be elected praetor or consul was not a noble, but his sons and all his direct male descendants were. Thus the attainment of office automatically ennobled a family, and the nobility consisted of the group of families which had thus been ennobled. These families soon came to feel that their members had a right to hold in due time the offices which their ancestors had held, that a consul's son should be elected consul in his turn when he reached the proper age. Animated by such feelings, the nobles exerted all their influence to keep the offices within their own circle and to keep "new men," as they called non-nobles, from being elected. In this they were so successful that they came to form a ring of four or five hundred families among whom the offices were passed around generation after generation. Of course their monopoly was never quite complete, for new men did occasionally make their way to the front, but when this happened, the new man merely became the founder of a new noble family, which was promptly assimilated to the rest. Such additions to the governing ring were inevitable because some of the old noble families died out in the course of time or sank into obscurity from various causes, and probably the new families that joined the circle did little more than replace those that disappeared.

In theory the Roman people could elect whom they pleased as magistrates; in fact they chose them almost exclusively from a small group of families. What is the explanation of such a condition? The usual answer of historians is that the nobility had a strong class consciousness and that their united influence was great enough to secure the result at which they aimed. In itself this is obviously no explanation, because the question is not whether the nobility was powerful, a fact of which there is no sort of doubt, but why they were powerful, and no explanation of their influence which seems really adequate has hitherto been given. We are told, in substance if not always in plain words, that the Romans were a deferential people who dearly loved a lord and had a profound respect for the great families and that these families maintained a proud tradition of service to the state. Now there is no doubt some element of truth in this explanation, but if we examine the record of the nobility we shall find good reason to feel that it is far from solving the problem, for the nobles did not display such conspicuous disinterestedness and outstanding ability that we can explain their influence on moral grounds alone. They furnished the state with an abundant supply of incompetent magistrates and shaped its policy to serve their selfish interests, they appropriated most of the public land for themselves and opposed every attempt to use this land for the benefit of the poor. A much more satisfactory explanation lies in the assumption that the nobles had contrived to build up an organized political machine, by means of which they were able to maintain their ascendency. The history of the Roman Republic, if carefully examined, will furnish sufficient evidence that such a machine existed and will make clear, at least in a general way, how it worked in practice. While the subject cannot be discussed here in detail,[1] a brief description of the machine is indispensable.

Since the assembly elected the magistrates and the ex-magistrates formed the senate, it is obvious that the control of the assembly was essential, and the organization of the assembly was such that it was comparatively easy for an organized minority to control it. Unlike the Greeks, the Romans in their assembly did not vote by individuals but by groups, and group voting always lends itself to manipulation. In Rome there were two distinct assemblies, the assembly of centuries and the assembly of tribes. The two did not differ in their composition, for every citizen had the right to attend both, but the difference lay wholly in the groups by which the vote was taken. The centuries were little used except for the election of the consuls and praetors, and, since they were subdivisions of the tribes, much the same considerations will apply to them as to the tribes and it is unnecessary to deal with them here. The tribes were the really basic group and originally they were territorial divisions; the earliest ones were very small in size, somewhat like our modern wards and townships. The city of Rome was divided into four tribes or wards, and the country around the city into some sixteen rural tribes or townships. As the power of Rome grew and her territory expanded new rural tribes were organized until there were finally thirty-one such tribes, which with the four city tribes gave a total of thirty-five. The later tribes were all rural, and they were larger in size and most of them farther from Rome than the original sixteen.

-----

[1]For a fuller discussion see my book *A History of the Roman World from 146 to 30 B.C.* (Methuen and Co., London, 1935; reprinted by The Macmillan Co., New York, 1939).

The members of a tribe were those citizens who resided within its boundaries.

In the tribal assembly, which passed laws and elected all magistrates except the censors, consuls, and praetors, each tribe had one vote and how that vote should be cast was determined by the members of the tribe who happened to be present on any given occasion, regardless of how many or how few those members were. At a meeting of the assembly the people gathered in a large open space around the sides of which there were a number of enclosures, one for each tribe. When the time came for taking the vote the members of each tribe went to the proper enclosure and when they were all within it, they came out again through the single opening, at each side of which a teller was stationed. As they passed out, each citizen gave his vote to the tellers, who counted the votes and informed the presiding magistrate how the tribe had voted, the votes of eighteen tribes being sufficient to elect a candidate or to decide the fate of a bill. When the result had been announced by the presiding magistrate, the assembly dispersed.

It may be well to repeat that the number of citizens voting in a tribe made absolutely no difference; five farmers from a rural tribe had exactly the same influence on the final decision as five thousand artisans from one of the urban tribes. The consequence of this was that the city rabble *never* controlled the action of the assembly, no matter how greatly they might outnumber the farmers at its meetings. In early times this had great advantages, because the country folk, although they were a large majority of the Roman people, could not attend the meetings of the assembly as easily or regularly as those who lived in the city, and the system of group voting prevented the state from falling under the control of the urban minority. There was, however, another side to the picture. The system enabled the rural minority of those present to outvote the urban

majority, but it also enabled a minority of that minority to
control the assembly. At least eleven of the rural tribes were
situated so far from Rome that very few small farmers from
them were likely to attend the assembly, and in some of those
near Rome it is probable that in comparatively early times a
few large landowners acquired most of the land and the small
farmers practically disappeared. From many of the rural
tribes, therefore, the attendance was likely to be small, and a
powerful political machine could easily be organized if some
means could be found of packing these tribes. By the end of
the fourth century B.C. membership in the tribes ceased to
depend upon residence, so that it became possible for certain
classes of people living in Rome to be registered in the rural
tribes. Originally this privilege seems to have been limited to
landowners, who were allowed to register themselves in any
tribe in which they owned land. Later certain classes among
the urban populace managed in practice to secure registration
in the rural tribes. When these changes had taken place, it
became possible for the wealthy landowners who resided in
Rome to have themselves registered in the rural tribes and to
form groups of retainers among the city poor who were also
registered in these tribes. These retainers, who were usually
either clients or freedmen, were expected by their patron to
vote in accordance with his wishes. Since the nobles were
mostly large landowners, the situation was obviously very much
to their advantage, and through their retainers, living in Rome
and so always on hand to vote in the assembly, they were able
to get a strong grip on many of the more thinly attended rural
tribes until at last they were able to control a majority of the
tribes. They thus succeeded in building up a well organized
political machine, which was the material basis on which
their ascendency rested. The development of this machine was
gradual, but long before the conquest of Italy was completed,

it had become so powerful that the assembly only escaped from its control at rare intervals.

It must be remembered that the machine was never quite secure against a temporary defeat under special conditions. Its mastery of the assembly was based on the small attendance of genuine rural voters in a majority of the country tribes, but there was always the possibility that on some particular occasion they would come to Rome in unusual numbers. If this happened, they might upset all calculations and elect some candidate who had aroused their enthusiasm or pass some bill in which they felt a keen interest. Such defeats, however, although they might be very unpleasant to the nobles, seldom had any really serious consequences. The country voters could not remain in the city, nor could they return often. After winning a victory over the machine, they had to go home again, and the machine could usually contrive to make their victory a fruitless one. If a candidate objectionable to the nobles was elected to office, he could probably accomplish little or nothing in a year, and if a law was passed of which the machine disapproved, it was generally possible to prevent its enforcement as soon as the excitement had died down. The machine was always on the spot and under normal conditions was sure to have a majority in the assembly. It would not often venture to try to repeal an obnoxious law, for so direct and obvious a move might anger the country voters and bring them back again; it was safer and generally quite as effective to elect magistrates who would make no effort to enforce it. Occasional defeats, therefore, did not seriously damage the machine or prevent it from carrying out its policy, and for between one and two hundred years the nobles were able to govern the Republic very much as they pleased.

If some harsh things have been said of the Roman nobility, it was only for the purpose of denying that they were a body of supermen, ruling by reason of exceptional virtue and capacity. Certainly there is no reason to think that they were more selfish or more stupid than any other governing class which the Romans could have found, and a governing class of some sort was a necessity. The constitution of the Republic provided so many checks and balances, so many opportunities for obstruction and deadlock, that in order to make it work at all some extra-constitutional power was required to give a certain degree of coherence and continuity to the policy of the state, and this power could hardly be found except by leaving the actual control of the government in the hands of a group of men capable of working together with a fair degree of harmony. The public business could be transacted only if the annual magistrates were willing to co-operate, or were somehow prevented from carrying their differences of opinion so far as to produce a deadlock. Such unity would be most easily secured if there existed some sort of organized parties by which the magistrates could be elected and to which they could be held accountable for their conduct in office. In fact the nobility formed such a party and they were the only party which had an effective organization capable of continuous and steady action, and in this we have the real explanation of their long supremacy.

The nobles, then, acquired power by building up a political machine, and they were able to do this by forming groups of retainers in the thinly attended rural tribes and in this way securing control, under normal circumstances, of the popular assembly. If they were to retain power, it was essential that they should work together without serious dissensions among themselves. This they were able to do because they had common economic interests. In early times almost the only form of investment for capital, and so almost the only form of wealth,

was land and slaves wherewith to work it. Thus at first the
only rich Romans were the large landowners and the nobility
was simply the most powerful section of this class, and they
continued to be a group of large landowners as long as the
Republic lasted. From the start they had an obvious motive for
desiring to control the government in order to direct its policy
in accordance with their class interests. As Rome conquered
her neighbors she acquired large tracts of public land, the
disposition of which was one of the chief political issues in the
early history of the Republic. If the great landowners had
control, they could deal with the public land so that in one
way or another they could get possession of it and add it to
their estates, but, if the poor were able to dictate the policy to
be pursued, they would divide it among themselves. To gain
power was, therefore, to the direct economic advantage of the
great landowners and by means of their retainers they were successful. Once power had been secured it was necessary to keep
it, for the poor were ever present and were always inclined to
favor legislation of a highly objectionable sort. Their class
interests, therefore, bound the nobles together in a compact
group and inspired them with a determination to preserve their
ascendency at all costs. Of course such motives were joined
with many others, and the nobles did not avow them even to
themselves in their direct and stark simplicity. It is always
easy for an aristocracy to persuade itself of its superiority, and
the Roman nobility was no exception; it soon came to believe
sincerely in its fitness and its almost divine right to govern the
Republic.

To maintain their control it was necessary for the nobles to
present a united front and they shaped the development of the
Roman constitution with that end in view. The senate was the
obvious body through which the nobility could most readily

govern, and it was naturally enough utilized and exalted. Since
the nobles monopolized the magistracies, they automatically
filled the senate, most of the noble families having at least one
member among the conscript fathers. The senate was thus
admirably adapted to serve the purpose of a party caucus where
questions of policy could be conveniently discussed and decided,
and a decision once reached was generally accepted and upheld
by the entire aristocracy. The political machine which the
nobles had built up and by which they controlled the assembly
was always at the disposal of the senate; it was in fact a
senatorial machine, and the supremacy of the senate ultimately
depended upon it. Since the magistrates were really named by
the machine, a uniform and coherent policy could be secured
under the direction of the senate in spite of the fact that the
men in office were constantly changed, and there was little
risk that differences of opinion among the magistrates would
become serious.

Clumsy as the structure of the government was, it could be
made to work with some degree of efficiency as long as the
senate's supremacy remained unquestioned. But since internal
unity was essential to the success of the machine, it was necessary to preserve it at all costs, and efficiency must sometimes be
sacrificed to harmony. When Rome annexed provinces outside
Italy, she was forced to provide governors for them, and these
governorships became the great prizes of public life. The system ultimately adopted was to send the consuls and praetors to
the provinces as governors for the year following their term of
office, the province which each should hold being determined by
lot. At first glance such a method seems remarkable in its
stupidity, for the accident of lot might send a successful lawyer
without military experience to suppress a formidable insurrection in Spain, while despatching a competent soldier to Sicily

where there was at the moment no trouble at all.   The system, however, had one enormous advantage for the machine, though it was responsible for more than one serious disaster to Rome. If the senate had undertaken to distribute the provinces among the consuls and praetors, the unity of the senatorial machine would almost certainly have been destroyed.   The different families of the nobility would have combined in cliques and intrigued against each other to secure the best provinces for themselves or for their friends and relatives, and, whatever arrangements were made, many families would have been left nursing a grievance and convinced that they had been unfairly treated.   The use of the lot removed such causes of friction within the governing class; each noble family was assured its fair chance at the prizes of official life and none was allowed more than its fair chance.   If a praetor received a poor province it was luck and not the intrigues of some rival family that was responsible, so that no lasting resentment was engendered. There seems no reasonable doubt that the lot was an important factor in maintaining the unity of the senatorial machine and that a more efficient system would have broken up the nobility into contending factions.

There was another direction in which the necessity of holding the governing families together was fatal to efficiency.   As long as it could command an important block of votes, each family must be given its chance at the offices and little attention could be paid to the personal character or ability of its candidate.   If the family lost its property, either by bad management or extravagance, it might be promptly relegated to obscurity because, when it could no longer keep its retainers, it ceased to be of value to the senatorial machine, but, until it could be dropped overboard entirely, it could not safely be ignored. Thousands of Roman lives were sacrificed to the blundering of stupid or inexperienced nobles elected to high office because of family influence and assigned to the command of an unfortunate army by the accident of lot. It was part of the price Rome had to pay for the privilege of being governed by the senatorial machine. In fairness, however, we should not forget that the machine was not without its merits. Under the senate the government did work after a fashion and without it we may reasonably doubt whether it could have worked at all. In spite of its manifest shortcomings and of repeated disasters the senate always contrived to muddle on to final success, and made Rome mistress first of Italy and then of the Mediterranean world. These are very solid and conspicuous achievements, which must be put down to the credit of the nobility. It seems certain that no other class in the Roman state would have accomplished more or governed better in the long run. If there were many stupid and unworthy nobles, there were also many of exceptional ability and high character, men who served their country well and honestly according to their lights and who repaired much of the damage which the others had caused.

While the nobility won for Rome the empire of the Mediterranean world, it should be added that this was done more or less involuntarily, for the nobility was not imperialistic and had no love of foreign conquest. The nobles as a class were rich landowners whose interests were bound up in their great estates in Italy. To secure the safety of those estates they wished to protect Italy against any danger from abroad, but they had little or no desire to undertake the government of people outside the peninsula, because they had little or no interest in this. The desire to be safe at home was the chief motive which led them to annex the first provinces abroad, and they strove to limit their responsibilities as much as possible. Events, however, proved stronger than their reluctance, and, once an empire had been established, it continued to grow in spite of them. In the preceding chapter it was pointed out that the demands of the empire put an intolerable strain on the old military system of the Republic and forced the government to employ proletarian armies, which it soon found itself unable to control. The problem thus created would not have been insoluble if the senatorial machine had remained securely intrenched at home. The growth of the empire, however, brought about economic and social changes which undermined the power of the machine. How this came about must now be considered very briefly.

We have seen how the expansion of Rome proved disastrous to the small farmers of Italy. The result was that many of them were ruined and either became a part of the rural proletariat, working as farm laborers or renting land from their more prosperous neighbors, or drifted to the cities, especially Rome, where they picked up a precarious livelihood as best they could. At first these developments were all to the advantage of the senatorial machine, for no attempt seems to have been made to change the registration of voters when they changed their residence. The nobles were able to increase the size of their country estates at small expense, and they could readily find clients among the ruined farmers who had moved to Rome but were still registered in the rural tribes where they had originally resided. For a time, therefore, conquest abroad served to strengthen the machine at home, and in the period of the great wars it reached the summit of its power. But the ruin of the small farmers could not be arrested when it ceased to be advantageous to the machine, and they continued to drift to Rome in such numbers that it was impossible to make clients of them all. Those who did not become retainers of the nobles merged with the city rabble, retaining like the clients their membership in the rural tribes. Gradually there developed a section of the urban proletariat which voted in the rural tribes but was not under the control of the nobles, and as a result the city rabble acquired an increasing influence in politics.

As the urban proletariat grew in number and in power, it grew also poorer and more miserable. Rome was not a great industrial or commercial center, so that it was impossible to find steady employment for more than a limited number. In the course of time the situation was bound to become such that the intervention of the state would be more or less inevitable, and the statesman who took the first important step in this direction was C. Gracchus. His famous corn law, by which grain was to be sold to the poor at about half the market price, has been bitterly condemned by many historians. Today it may appear in a somewhat different light as neither more nor less than a measure of unemployment relief. Whatever his motives in proposing it, the law once passed became an established institution, perhaps for political reasons, but, perhaps, because unemployment proved to be a permanent and not a temporary condition and one which grew worse rather than better with time. In any case it was a misfortune for the senate that the first steps for the benefit of the poor were taken by a political opponent. C. Gracchus, like his brother, was killed (121 B.C.), but his tragic fate only alienated the mob more than ever. His career seems to have impressed upon the rabble the conviction that they could hope for nothing from the senate and to have created an antagonism between the machine and a large and growing section of the urban poor. In time the city mob might have gained sufficient power to dominate the assembly and so to control the government, if it had not been balanced by the development of another class.

The growth of Rome's power abroad inevitably gave a great impetus to business and opened up new opportunities for wealth, of which Roman capitalists promptly availed themselves. Every new province was a new field where any man with ready money could find profitable investments. There had always been men in Rome who instead of buying land preferred to engage in various business enterprises, such as commerce or government contracting, but as a class such men did not become very important until the period of expansion began. Expansion abroad led to a rapid increase in their number and wealth, so that they ultimately became a rich and influential class known by the somewhat curious name of the *equites* or knights. They carried on trade, acted as bankers, loaned money to provincial towns, leased mines and other public properties, formed syndicates, or companies, which took contracts for all kinds of public works and farmed the taxes, in short they engaged in all sorts of business. Many of their enterprises were perfectly legitimate, but many of them were at least open to question, and it soon became obvious to them that the attitude of a provincial governor or of the magistrates in Rome might have a considerable influence upon their profits, legitimate or otherwise. In other words they found that political power could be exceedingly useful to them. They had no desire to hold the offices themselves, but they did desire to be able to put pressure upon the nobles who did. The knights, then, after a time began to seek some means of influencing the policy of the state and of compelling its agents and representatives to act in accordance with their interests. This was natural enough, and the means of acquiring such influence were ready to their hands, for the nobles had no monopoly of the methods by which they had built up their machine. Any Roman with enough wealth could form a group of retainers voting in some of the rural tribes exactly as the nobles had done. It was, therefore, perfectly easy for the knights to organize a political machine of their own precisely similar to that of the nobles, and they soon began to do so. At first, no doubt, it was on a somewhat modest scale, but even so it was probably capable of making itself felt, since at almost every election there were more candidates than there were offices, the nobles never having eliminated a certain amount of competition among themselves.

As the wealth of the knights grew, the strength of their machine steadily increased, until finally the great landowners found themselves face to face with big business. Much would obviously depend on the relations between the two organized sets of special interests: would they fight each other, or would they combine to keep the city rabble from gaining power? The answer is that they did neither consistently and both intermittently. The nobles clung to power and tried to run the government to suit themselves as they had been doing for so long, but with less and less success, although they had a great advantage in the fact that the knights appear to have been frequently divided among themselves. Even when united the capitalists could never actually control the assembly without forming an alliance with the rabble, and such an alliance generally had to be paid for in some fashion. There was no real sympathy between the rabble and the knights, for the two classes had few if any interests in common, so it was practically impossible for them to co-operate except for short periods and to a limited extent. On the other hand, as men of property the knights on many matters held the same views as the great landowners; both looked with strong disfavor on anything which disturbed or threatened the security and rights of property, although some measures would affect one class much more seriously than the other. On the whole, the knights could work more frequently with the nobles than with the rabble, but a permanent alliance proved impossible because the interests of the capitalists occasionally clashed with those of the landowners. The actual situation which ultimately developed was that the senatorial machine could no longer control the assembly if the knights and the rabble combined against it. Usually a sufficiently large section of the knights was willing to support the senate, but from time to time the capitalists became so much exasperated at the senate's conduct of the government that they offered some concession to the rabble and so secured the support of the mob for an attack upon the senate. Such an alliance, however, could not last long because the rabble soon began to demand more than the knights were willing to concede, and the capitalists, having got what they wanted, were ready to allow the nobles, humiliated and punished, to regain the outward possession of power. Under such conditions constructive statesmanship was practically impossible; all that could be done was to meet the difficulties of the moment by hasty compromises or temporary expedients. The senate was too weak to solve the vital problems of the day, so that breakdown of constitutional government might be delayed but could no longer be prevented.

III

THE BREAKDOWN OF CONSTITUTIONAL GOVERNMENT

In the last day of the Republic we have seen that the most vital problem confronting the government was to find some means of recovering control of the army, but by the time that this problem arose the political instability had become so great as to make a successful handling of it almost impossible. A brief consideration of the ways in which the problem might have been solved will suffice to make this point sufficiently clear.

The most effective solution of the military problem would have been to establish an adequate standing army and at the same time a special fund to provide land for the soldiers when their term of service expired. In fact this was precisely the policy adopted by Augustus with excellent results, but such a solution seems never to have been considered under the Republic. The idea of maintaining a larger standing army than was required by the immediate and pressing needs of the state was contrary to the Roman tradition, and it may be doubted whether in any case the treasury could have met the heavy expenditure involved. It is impossible to determine accurately what the revenues of Rome amounted to at any given time, but a reasonable estimate for the period from 80 to 62 B.C. would be from \$8,000,000 to \$10,000,000 a year, much the greater part of which came from the tribute of the provinces.[1] From this income the state had to meet all administrative expenses, the cost of any public works which might be undertaken, the charge of the corn dole in Rome, and the payment of the army. By the time of Augustus the revenues had been greatly increased, partly by the conquests of Pompey and Caesar, but above all by the annexation of Egypt. Yet even with these added resources the expense of maintaining an adequate standing army weighed very heavily on the treasury and was only met with difficulty. Whether the Republic could have adopted this method of solving the problem may be doubted, but there were political as well as financial obstacles in the way. It seems certain that a large standing army could have been maintained only by rigorous economy in every other direction, and such economy was certain to be unpopular not only with the politicians but with large numbers of the voters as well. The expenditure of the state was normally determined by the senate, but, even if the senate had conceived and attempted to carry out the policy of Augustus, it seems certain that under the conditions prevailing in the last years of the Republic the attempt would have met with no success, as a brief consideration of some of these conditions will show.

The mob, of course, always favored a lavish expenditure on games and on the corn dole, but by itself it could not enforce its wishes. If it could have done so, there can be little doubt that it would have gotten its grain for nothing long before the tribuneship of Clodius (58 B.C.). Helpless by itself, it became dangerous if joined by many discontented nobles and knights. Among the knights many were engaged in contracting for

---

[1]See Tenney Frank, *An Economic Survey of Ancient Rome:* vol. I, *Rome and Italy of the Republic* (Baltimore, The Johns Hopkins Press, 1933), pp. 322–24.

public works and would not desire to see the government re-
trench in this direction, while many nobles were ready to fight
for large appropriations for administrative purposes. Perhaps
this element among the nobles was the most important single
factor in the situation. Under the Republic neither the magistrates nor the provincial governors were paid any regular
salaries. There was, moreover, no legitimate way in which
the magistrate could make money out of his office; in fact the
service of the state was at once honorable and costly. Such
being the case, the government came to regard it as both
natural and proper that those who served the state at their
own expense at home should have a chance to recover what
they had spent, and perhaps much more, as governors of the
provinces. Although the governor received no salary, the
senate gave him a certain allowance for the necessary administrative expenses and the pay of the troops stationed in
the province. If the allowance proved to be larger than was
needed, it was regarded as right and proper for the governor
to keep the unexpended balance instead of turning it back to
the treasury. There were, therefore, many nobles strongly in
favor of a policy of liberal allowances for governors, and in
general the senate showed little, if any, disposition to practice
economy in a field where generosity was becoming a matter of
very serious importance to a considerable section of the governing class. For a long time a political career had been growing more and more expensive, with the consequence that many
of those who reached the higher offices had to borrow heavily
to do so and could only hope to pay their debts by the profits
of a provincial governorship.

The reasons why candidates for office were forced to spend
more and more lavishly are to some extent a matter of conjecture, but the chief cause was in all probability the steady

growth of the urban rabble and especially that section of it which voted in the rural tribes but was not controlled by either the knights or the nobles.   When not stirred by any strong emotion, this element seems to have been ready enough to accept bribes. Certainly bribery was nothing new in Rome, but, as the power of the city mob increased, it came to be practiced on such a scale that many of the successful politicians found themselves much embarrassed financially if not practically ruined.   Under such conditions a very considerable number of the senators would be certain to favor liberal appropriations for the governors and to resist any attempt to increase the size of the regular army beyond the obvious needs of the moment, since such an increase would have to be paid for out of the appropriations and would inevitably diminish the possible profits of the governors.   Nor was it an easier matter to accumulate a large reserve in the treasury to enable the state to provide for such special armies as might have to be raised, for such a reserve could only be created by the same sort of economy.   If the senate adopted this policy, the only result might be to provoke a coalition of discontented elements to take the control of the treasury out of the senate's hands, at least until the reserve had been squandered.   This danger could not be ignored because, although the senate normally had charge of the finances of the Republic, the assembly could at any time make such special appropriations as it pleased in spite of the senate's opposition.

It was, therefore, practically impossible for the Republic to attempt the solution which proved successful under the Empire. There was, however, another method of dealing with the problem which might have yielded good results; this was for the senate to make a serious effort to provide for each special army in turn.   If the men had been taught by experience that they could expect liberal treatment from the senate without the need of any pressure on the part of their general, it might have been possible for the senate to secure a real hold upon them. Instead of pursuing this course the senate did almost the exact opposite and succeeded in convincing the soldiers that only through their general could they hope for anything at all. Such a policy amounted to suicide and the fall of the Republic was the natural and inevitable consequence, but, although we cannot acquit the nobles of blundering very badly, it is possible to explain to some extent how they came to blunder. To do this it is necessary to examine briefly their handling of one or two critical situations.

The first of these situations arose in 100 B.C. Marius had just beaten the Cimbri and Teutones with an army which certainly contained a large number of volunteers attracted by the promise of land. The troops must be disbanded and provision made for them. Probably the critical nature of the occasion was not in the least realized, for volunteer armies were an innovation and their character had yet to be revealed. Marius naturally was anxious to redeem his promises; his plan apparently was to found colonies for his soldiers in the provinces, and he wished to be consul for the sixth time in 100 B.C. so that this policy could be carried out under his own supervision and to his own glory. The nobles were naturally, but very unfortunately, exasperated, and, so far from being willing to let him have a sixth consulship, they were extremely anxious to get rid of him altogether. He was a new man, a vulgar commoner, and his rise to power had been a particularly humiliating defeat for the nobility. The war against Jugurtha had furnished him an opportunity of which he had taken full and not over-polite advantage. The whole affair of Jugurtha had been thoroughly disastrous to the senate. As a matter of fact there is much to be said for the senate's policy, which was to keep out of a war in Africa at almost any cost; serious danger was threatening on the northern frontier, and all the available soldiers might be needed for defense, while a war with Jugurtha could yield no advantage whatever to Rome, at least from the standpoint of the nobles. The senate, however, contrived to mismanage matters, offending the patriotic emotions of the rabble and ignoring the interests of the knights. The result was an explosion, and big business in alliance with the mob drove the senate into a war which proved much longer and more serious than the critics of the senate had expected. When the senate's generals failed to gain any impressive success, public opinion again became irritated. In this irritation Marius, who had been serving in Africa, saw his opportunity and he returned to Rome to become a candidate for the consulship. The knights and the people were alike disgusted with aristocratic generals who had apparently accomplished little or nothing, and Marius was elected consul for 107 B.C. and given charge of the war. He seems to have followed the same strategy as his predecessor, Metellus, and finally succeeded in ending the war, as Metellus would probably have done if let alone. The nobles bitterly resented the way Marius had been thrust upon them and they were not impressed by his success, but they were unable to get rid of him. While he was in Africa, Roman arms had met with a series of disasters in Gaul, which culminated in an appalling defeat at Arausio, where the Cimbri and Teutones destroyed two Roman armies (105 B.C.). Italy lay open to invasion, and Marius seemed indispensable to everybody except the nobles, perhaps even to them. The law forbade re-election to the consulship, but it was set aside in favor of the rough soldier who had risen from the ranks. The Cimbri and Teutones failed to follow up their

victory at Arausio, but Marius was re-elected year after year
to organize the defense and to meet them when they should
come. They finally came in 101 B.C. and Marius annihilated
them, so that at length Rome breathed freely once more. To
the nobles there seemed now no reason whatever to elect Marius
consul again, but he thought differently. Since he could expect
no support from the senatorial machine, he allied himself with
two reckless politicians who were bitter opponents of that
machine and were cordially hated by the nobles. He was
triumphantly elected consul for the sixth time and attempted
with the help of his allies to carry out his plan for rewarding
his army. The senate seems to have opposed the bill brought
forward for this purpose; probably it cared little about the bill
itself but was actuated by aversion to the men who proposed it.
The result was unfortunate, because on the first occasion when
a volunteer army confronted the senate, the soldiers found that
body fighting strenuously against their demands, so that whatever they received they obviously owed to the influence of their
general. This particular case has been considered at greater
length than it deserves, perhaps, because it shows the way in
which the problem of providing for an army always got entangled in politics, so that the question could not be settled on
its merits and the issues were more or less obscured. It was
probably for this reason that the senate blundered so badly,
then and subsequently. The majority of the senators were
unable to rise above the party politics of the moment to the
level of real statesmanship.

For some years after 100 B.C. the Roman government was
concerned with other matters than the new armies. The chief
question was the demand of the Italians for full citizenship,
which led to the Social War (90–88 B.C.) and afterwards to
violent dissensions in Rome, wherein both sides resorted to

violence. We may pass over these struggles, since the military problem was so involved with other issues that the senate's attitude was of comparatively little importance. In the end Sulla at the head of one of the new armies crushed all opposition and made himself dictator of Rome (82 B.C.). Since he happened to belong to the senatorial party, he used his power to entrench the senate in control and endeavored by a series of ingeniously contrived laws to make any interference with its government legally impossible for the future. He found land for his soldiers by a wholesale massacre of his defeated opponents accompanied by the confiscation of their property. His measures, however, had no permanent effect, for the senate was unable to maintain the control which he had given it and was soon compelled to sanction the repeal of his most important laws. The cause of this counter-revolution was very simple. Sulla had established the supremacy of the senate with the help of one volunteer army, and Pompey overthrew its supremacy with the help of another. In reality the soldiers cared nothing for the senate in either case and simply followed their general.

After Sulla's death (78 B.C.) Pompey was the leading military man in Rome. He had been one of Sulla's lieutenants in the recent civil war and had acquired a reputation and a popularity which seem to have been somewhat beyond his real deserts. Whether he had any serious political convictions it is impossible to say with certainty; he may have been a moderate man who disliked extremes on either side. Such a man might join Sulla when he returned from the East and yet have been disgusted at the manner in which he used, or abused, his victory. In any case there can be no doubt that Pompey was eager for glory and distinction. Sulla perceived clearly that the ambition of his young lieutenant would never be satisfied by the humdrum career which he had planned for the members of the governing oligarchy and so set him down as a man not to be trusted. After Sulla's death the senate which he left in power apparently inherited his view of Pompey as a dangerous man, but circumstances forced the nobles to make use of him in spite of themselves. Hardly was Sulla's funeral over when his opponents, who had seemed completely crushed, rose in revolt, and the senate in a panic eagerly accepted Pompey's offer of his services. The young general had no difficulty in raising an army and the rebellion was easily suppressed. This success, however, was not enough to satisfy Pompey's thirst for glory, so he suggested that the senate send him to Spain to assist in putting down a formidable insurrection there under a leader named Sertorius. The conscript fathers regarded Pompey with undiminished suspicion, but he was at the head of an army in Italy, and to get rid of him they agreed to his suggestion. This policy was successful for the moment, but when Sertorius was disposed of (72 B.C.) a new crisis arose.

During Pompey's absence in Spain there was an outbreak of slaves in Italy (73 B.C.), which forced the senate to put another unreliable general, the millionaire Crassus, in command of an army. Like Pompey, Crassus had been a lieutenant of Sulla, and, like Pompey again, he had aroused the suspicions of the dictator and been relegated to private life. There he remained, occupying his leisure in amassing wealth, until the servile uprising had become so formidable a menace that the senate had no alternative but to call upon the one competent military man available to save society. The choice was justified by the result, for Crassus was successful, but there were times when the issue appeared doubtful, and in a moment of discouragement the terrified senate called Pompey home to help him, so that there were two armies in Italy under generals neither of whom had any real loyalty to the senate. The two generals, however, happened to dislike each other, and the senate probably imagined that it could take advantage of this fact to thwart them both.   Pompey might have been easily conciliated, for his demands seem to have been such as could have been granted without serious difficulty.   He doubtless wished to provide for his soldiers, and he certainly wished to be consul.   His men apparently could be satisfied with allotments in Spain, where the insurrection had furnished ample excuse for seizing as much land as was needed, and, although Pompey was not legally eligible for the consulship, the senate could have sanctioned a dispensation in his favor.   However, the nobles had no desire to bestow any special privileges or distinctions on Pompey, and they seem to have believed that Crassus would support them in their refusal.   It was a complete miscalculation; Crassus disliked Pompey, but he likewise wanted the consulship and thought that he had little chance of getting it through the senatorial machine.   Accordingly he threw the senate overboard and made a bargain with Pompey, who agreed to take him as his colleague.   With their armies they easily overawed the senate, and to provide popular enthusiasm they allied themselves with the knights and the rabble, agreeing to repeal such of Sulla's laws as were obnoxious to these classes. Without difficulty they undid the measures by which Sulla had fortified the power of the senate (70 B.C.), and they got rid of their armies in some fashion, though unfortunately the details are lacking on this point.

The failure to concede Pompey's demands had cost the senate all the special defenses which Sulla had given it, but it still remained the governing body of the Republic, although its control was open to challenge at any time.   The chief beneficiaries by the consulship of Pompey and Crassus were the knights, whose influence in politics Sulla had destroyed but who now recovered their old position and once more held the balance of power. It was not long before they intrusted two new commissions to Pompey, first that of suppressing piracy in the Mediterranean (67 B.C.) and then that of carrying on a war in the East against Mithridates, king of Pontus (66 B.C.). The senate was opposed, but with the knights and the rabble united the aristocratic machine was powerless. For four years Pompey was absent in the East; when his work there was finished, a crisis began which was fatal to the Republic. The senate had a chance, its last chance, to win the confidence of the army, and it threw that chance away.

When Pompey brought the war with Mithridates to an end, he was potentially the master of the Roman world, for he was at the head of an irresistible army. For several years most Roman politicians had foreseen more or less clearly that sooner or later this situation would arise and had been asking themselves in nervous apprehension what Pompey would do. What he did do when the time came seems to have taken many of them by surprise. Instead of making himself dictator, as they had feared, he quietly disbanded his army and returned to Rome a private citizen (62 B.C.). Some modern historians have been equally astonished at his conduct and have wasted time and ingenuity in unnecessary explanations. The simple fact seems to be that Pompey had no desire to be dictator and therefore made no effort to become one. What he wanted was something quite different, and something which he thought that he could get without serious difficulty. For himself he wished to be the foremost citizen of the Republic, honored and respected by all, living a life of luxurious leisure except when some crisis called for the exercise of his pre-eminent abilities. Such a position he could hold only on condition that he now secured land for his disbanded veterans. If he did this, nothing could destroy his influence; no aristocratic intrigues could really affect him, and in spite of all his enemies could do, he would remain Rome's greatest general, the man to whom in time of danger all *must* turn to save the state.   His reputation was to some extent undeserved, but that did not matter in the least; his influence was due not to what he had done, but to what he was believed to have done, and in Rome he counted for what the rural proletariat of Italy imagined him to be.   The one thing that could seriously diminish his greatness would be failure to provide for his veterans, for this was the one thing that would destroy the magic of his name throughout the countryside; the next time he called for volunteers he might call in vain, and a Pompey who could not raise an army in Italy by a word would be a Pompey who did not particularly matter in Rome.   If he did not wish to risk a permanent eclipse, he must at all costs provide for his former soldiers. Pompey was not an astute politician, but considerations so obvious can hardly have escaped him.   Even if he was only dimly conscious of them, he had a sufficient sense of honor to feel himself under the strongest obligation to those who had faced danger and endured hardship in reliance on his promises. Probably, when he disbanded his army, he imagined that he could readily provide for his men without violating the law or making himself dictator, but he soon discovered his mistake.

The problem of providing for his army was the most difficult that the Republic had ever been called upon to face.   The war against Mithridates had been fought in the interior of Asia Minor, where the soldiers were unwilling to settle, so that the land must be found in Italy.   Pompey had a plan, which was probably the best which could be devised under the circumstances.   In the East he had annexed two new provinces which would pay a large tribute, and he proposed to set aside this tribute for a period of five years to form a special fund to be used to purchase land for his men. In addition he proposed to distribute among them a considerable tract of land which the state still owned in Campania. A tribune friendly to Pompey brought a bill embodying these provisions before the senate. In the light of what followed it is easy to see that the wise course for the senate would have been to approve the bill, with some modifications perhaps, and to have thrown the whole influence of the aristocratic machine behind it in the assembly. By doing this the senate would have given an impressive demonstration not only to Pompey's veterans but to all future armies as well that it could be trusted to do everything in reason to satisfy their claims.

Perhaps the ablest leader of the senate at this time was Cicero; though he may not have understood all that was involved in the situation, he saw clearly enough that the question should be treated in a liberal spirit, and he tried to bring Pompey and the senate together. The nobles, however, refused to follow his lead. They objected to the allotment of the Campanian land on the ground that it yielded the chief revenue which was collected in Italy, so that if it were given up, the treasury would depend almost entirely on the receipts from the provinces, which an invasion or a rebellion might cut off at any time. With this objection Cicero agreed, but he was prepared to support the purchase part of the plan. His efforts were in vain, for the senate was opposed to the whole scheme, "believing," as Cicero wrote to his friend Atticus (i, 19), "that some new power for Pompey was aimed at." The meaning of these words may be readily guessed. To carry out the purchase and distribution of the land a commission would have to be set up, which would probably be dominated by Pompey.

This board would have a vast fund at its disposal and could so spend it as to influence the elections for several years to come, a possibility which was naturally very disturbing to all politicians who were, had been, or might be unfriendly to Pompey. We may doubt whether such apprehensions alone would have been enough to defeat the bill, even though they would unite all enemies of Pompey against it.   Behind all open objections and reinforcing all other motives was probably the old antagonism between Pompey and the senate.

It should be remembered that since the death of Sulla almost every step in Pompey's career had been a defeat and humiliation for the senate.   After his return from Spain he had compelled the nobles to concede him the consulship, and, as consul, had forced them to restore the privileges of the knights.   The commands against the pirates and against Mithridates had been given him by a coalition of the knights and the rabble, and the senate had been forced to acquiesce.   From the aristocratic point of view his rise had been a disaster and his continued influence meant trouble in the future.   The chance to weaken his prestige and popularity with the rural proletariat by refusing to let him provide for his veterans was tempting, and the senate yielded to the temptation.   The conscript fathers did not flatly reject the bill, but they could not be induced to approve it.   Pompey had it brought directly before the assembly, but it was soon apparent that it could not be passed. Even with the support of the senatorial machine it is very probable that the result would have been the same unless the senate was willing to make concessions in an entirely different matter in order to carry the bill.

Roman politics were at the moment in a state of confusion. In the preceding year the syndicate which had farmed the

taxes of the province of Asia had demanded that the price
which they had agreed to pay should be reduced by one-third.
The rejection of this demand by the senate of course angered
the capitalists involved, and with the help of a tribune they
might have blocked any measure favored by the senate until
their demands were granted.   It is, therefore, quite possible
that the senate could only have rewarded Pompey's veterans
by making a bargain with the knights which would have
seriously reduced the revenue from Asia.   The senate, however, had no wish to make disagreeable compromises for the
sake of a bill to which it was secretly opposed.   In the assembly
the senatorial machine was always against any measure brought
before the people without the senate's approval, and on this
matter it could count on the support of Crassus, who seldom
missed an opportunity to thwart Pompey and who controlled
a section of the rabble and the knights.   Perhaps, if brought
to a vote, the bill might have been carried in spite of all opposition, but the senate always had a tribune at hand to block
measures which could not be otherwise defeated, and Pompey
must soon have realized that his bill had no chance and apparently allowed it to drop.   Obviously the senate should have
made every effort to pass it and should have paid any price
necessary for that purpose.   To oppose it was certain to be
ruinous in the end, but the future was thrown away by men
blinded by the resentments and party squabbles of the moment.
If the senate had been in firm control of the government for
the past ten years such a situation could not have arisen, because
the nobles would have been able to prevent Pompey's getting
an army if they disliked or distrusted him, while, if they were
on friendly terms with him, they would have been able to
provide for his men without the necessity of bargains and
compromises.   As it was, the whole question had become en-

tangled in politics, and the senate was unable to find any solution which it was willing to accept, so that, while wrecking Pompey's bill, it proposed nothing in its place. This result was due largely to the past and present weakness of the aristocratic machine, but the consequence was that in the future no general and no army would be willing to trust the senate.

His defeat rendered Pompey so desperate that he was ready to grasp at any means to obtain land for his veterans. At this moment Julius Caesar appeared upon the scene as a candidate for the consulship (60 B.C.). He was well aware that, though he must expect the bitter opposition of the senatorial machine, he was personally popular and could count on the support of Crassus. To make his election certain he wished to secure the support of Pompey also. At the moment Crassus was at odds with the senate as well as with Pompey, and Caesar persuaded him that he would gain more by laying aside his private grudges and combining with Pompey than in any other way. On his side Pompey was probably ready to be reconciled with anybody in order to provide for his men. The combination is known in history as the First Triumvirate, although there is no evidence that it was so called by contemporaries. Caesar was elected, but his colleague in the consulship and several tribunes were adherents of the machine. In consequence he found himself as helpless as Pompey had been. He brought forward Pompey's bill again and the senate talked as interminably as before. Then he turned to the assembly. It seems clear that there was now a majority in favor of the bill if it could be brought to a vote, but a vote was rendered legally impossible by the vetoes of the other consul and three tribunes. The deadlock was apparently complete, but Caesar had no scruple about breaking the law, and Pompey had reached the point where he was ready to connive at its violation by someone else. With the support of his partners Caesar let loose the mob, which was, no doubt, largely reinforced by Pompey's veterans. His opponents were driven from the assembly, and he declared the bill duly enacted. Such a declaration was obviously false if any attention whatever was paid to the constitution, but the senate did not dare to annul the so-called law, for the Triumvirs had taken the precaution to provide Caesar with an army before he began his career of riotous illegality. During the remainder of his consulship Caesar was a dictator in all but name, the constitution was practically suspended, and the nobles watched his proceedings in helpless terror. Even when his term expired their fears were not at an end, because he had been assigned the province of Cisalpine Gaul for a term of years, a province from which he could march swiftly on Rome if the conduct of the senate made such a course necessary.

After Caesar's consulship in 59 B.C. the senate was never again really in control of the government. While he was busy in Gaul, his partners held it in check in Rome. There were moments when the hopes of the nobles rose high owing to the quarrels of Crassus and Pompey, but Caesar succeeded in bringing about another reconciliation (56 B.C.) and so prevented the senate from regaining power. Nevertheless, the Triumvirate could not continue indefinitely, and when Crassus was killed in the East (53 B.C.), where he had undertaken a war with Parthia, Pompey and Caesar began to drift apart. The conquest of Gaul was completed (51 B.C.) and the time was approaching when Caesar's army would have to be disbanded. He was naturally unwilling to imitate Pompey's example, having seen only too clearly the results of such a course. Whether he was ambitious or not, in this matter he probably had practically no choice. It is extremely unlikely that his soldiers would have consented to lay down their arms until they were safely provided with their farms, for Pompey's experience must have taught them the same lesson that it had taught Caesar. His demands were the very least that his army could safely permit him to make, and they were simply that he should hold the consulship a second time under conditions which would make him strong enough to reward his men, with or without the consent of the senate.

While such terms must have seemed moderate to him and his army, the nobles looked upon them in a very different light. The blood of the senators ran cold at the thought of a second consulship for Caesar, remembering as they did their experience of his first. Moreover, if he were powerful enough to enact the necessary laws to provide for his soldiers in defiance of the senate, it was obvious that he would be powerful enough to pass any other laws which he might happen to desire; in other words, he would be the absolute master of the state, and the aristocracy had no reason whatever to imagine that he would prove an agreeable master from their point of view. They were naturally alarmed at this prospect and Pompey soon began to share their fears. It is often said that Pompey grew jealous of Caesar's greatness and glory, which inevitably diminished his own. It is highly probably that such feelings influenced him to some extent, but we are hardly warranted in assuming that they were the chief motive in determining his course. Even if he had been able and willing to put aside all personal considerations, he would still have had sufficient cause to ally himself with the senate in opposition to Caesar, for unless he did so, he was practically assisting Caesar to establish a dictatorship, in fact if not in name. It must have seemed to him, therefore, that he had no choice except either to acquiesce in the overthrow of the Republic or to join those who were ready to make a desperate effort to avert its doom, and we can hardly be surprised that he decided on an alliance with the aristocracy. The least that the allies could demand was that, if Caesar were allowed a second consulship, it should be under such conditions that he could be held in check and compelled to keep within the limits of the Roman constitution. Such terms, however, would have left Caesar powerless to reward his men without the senate's consent, and that consent was something which he had no reason to expect from the record of the conscript fathers in the past. Hence to concede the demands of his opponents was to betray the interests of his army, and it is very unlikely that his soldiers would have permitted him to yield even if he had been disposed to do so to avert a civil war.

So complete a deadlock would never have developed if, after Pompey's return from the East, the nobles had followed Cicero's advice and supported some measure to provide for his veterans. Such a course could hardly have failed to draw Pompey into an alliance with the senate, with the result that the Triumvirate would never have been formed. Without the help of his part-ners Caesar would probably never have secured the command of a powerful army, and, even if he had secured one, his soldiers would have been less ready to fight for him against the state, because they would have felt some confidence in the senate. But men must reap the harvest of their own blunders, and the failure of the constitutional authorities to deal suc-cessfully with the volunteer armies could have only one result: sooner or later the army would set up a military dictatorship on the ruins of the Republic. If Pompey had won the Civil War, the end would at best simply have been postponed. His victory would have solved no problems and provided no security for the future, and before long some other general would have done the work of Caesar.

INDEX

(Prepared by Professor P. M. Batchelder)

Aegina, war with, 31
Agricultural depression, see Depression
Arausio, defeat at, 107f
Archons, 18, 20ff, 25f
Areopagus, 18ff, 22
Aristides, 31, 43f
Aristotle, Treatise on Athenian Constitution, 13, 15, 18, 22, 25; Politics, 25
Armies, Roman: reorganized by Marius, 61, 66; recruiting of, 61f, 66ff; size of, 62, 65, 77; length of service in, 62f, 75; volunteers for, 66ff, 77; attached to their generals, 67, 71, 73, 79, 106; proletarian character of, 67f, 97; as political arguments, 74, 78f, 111; old and new compared, 75f; standing army, 76ff, 102f, 105; special armies, 77ff; danger to Republic, 78f; overthrow Republic, 59ff, 120
Asia, province of, 116
Assembly, Athenian, 18ff, 40ff
Assembly, Roman: composition and powers of, 82f, 105; control of, 88, 89ff; method of voting, of, 40, 88f
Athens: depression in, 13ff; government of, 18ff, 40ff; prosperity of, 28, 30f; as head of Delian Confederacy, 33f; political parties in, 41ff; as imperial state, 30–51; as champion of democracy, 50f, 54
Attica, see Athens
Atticus, 114
Augustus, 102f

Black Sea region: wheat imported from, 14, 33, 50
Booty of war, 70f
Breakdown of constitutional government in Rome, 102–120
Bribery, 105

Caesar, Julius, 68, 103; forms First Triumvirate, 117; elected consul,
117; becomes practically dictator, 118; conquers Gaul, 118; demands second consulship, 119f
Campania, 114
Capitalists, see Knights
Cato, 69
Cicero, 114, 120
Cimbri, 72, 106, 107
City states, 38f, 46, 51ff, 59f
Civil war in Italy, 68, 73f, 109, 120
Cleisthenes, 30f, 42
Clodius, 103
Colonies of Athens, 49, 50
Conscription of Roman armies, 61ff, 66, 67 note, 75
Conservative party in Athens, 41f, 44, 47
Constitution, Roman, 81ff, 92, 93f, 118, 120
Consuls, 81, 83, 84, 86, 88, 94f
Corn dole, 103
Corn law of C. Gracchus, 98
Corruption, political, 59f, 105
Corsica, 73
Crassus, 116; crushes slave revolt, 74, 110; elected consul, 111; enters First Triumvirate, 117; death of, 118
Currency standards in Greece, 16
Cylon, 15

Darius, king of Persia, 31
Debts: slavery for, 14ff, 25, 27; Solon's cancellation of, 15f; of Roman politicians, 104
Delos, Confederacy of: organization of, 33f; success of, 34; transformed into Athenian Empire, 34–38; policy of Athens toward, 39f, 46f, 50f, 54
Democratic party in Athens, 41f, 44f, 47
Depression in Attica, 13ff; in Italy, 64f
Devaluation of drachma, 16f, 19

Dictatorships, 15, 27, 60
Draco, 15, 18, 26

Efficiency of Roman government, 94ff, 101
Egypt, 103
Empire, Athenian, 30, 32, 34f, 38, 48ff, 54f
Empire, Roman: expansion of, 61ff, 65, 96f, 99

Fall of Roman Republic, causes of, 59ff, 106, 116, 120
Farmers in Attica, 14; in Roman army, 62f, 65f; ruined by cheap grain, 64f; numbers increased by T. Gracchus, 66; rarely able to attend Roman assembly, 89ff
Farming of taxes, 63, 115f
Fleet, see Navy
Four Hundred, Council of, 18f, 22, 24f, 54
Frank, Tenney, 103 note

Gaul, Cisalpine, 68, 118
Gaul, Transalpine, 73, 118
Generals, Roman, 67, 70f, 76, 107
Gracchus, Gaius, 98
Gracchus, Tiberius, 66
Grain: raised in Attica, 14, 27f; imported from Black Sea region, 14, 33, 50; exportation prohibited, 17; from Sicily, 63f; fall of price in Italy, 64f; sold to poor at half price, 98; see also Corn dole, Corn law
Grapes, growing of, 27f, 64

Heliaea, 23ff
Hellespont, 35, 49
Hyperbolus, 44

Imperialism in Athens, 47, 49; in Rome, 65, 96

Jugurtha, war with, 66, 72, 76, 106f
Jury service in Athens, 48

Knights, Roman: become important class, 99; acquire political influence,
99f; hold balance of power, 100f, 103f; help provoke Jugurthan war, 107; join with Pompey and Crassus, 111; recover balance of power, 111f, 115; attitude toward Pompey's bill, 116

Land grants to soldiers, 68, 71ff, 79, 106, 108, 109, 111, 112ff, 119

Machine, political: built up by nobles, 87f; mode of operation of, 90f; uses lot to preserve harmony, 95; effects of ruin of farmers on, 97f; rival machine of knights, 99f; defeated by Marius, 108; defeated by knights and rabble, 112; weakness of, 117; blocks First Triumvirate, 117
Marathon, battle of, 31
Marius: reorganizes army, 61, 66; military career, 72, 106ff; political career, 106ff
Metellus, 107
Military service in Rome, 61
Mithridates, king of Pontus, 73, 75, 78, 112, 113
Mob, see Rabble
Mortgages, cancelled by Solon, 15

Navy, Athenian: and democracy, 30, 32; building of, 31f, 36f; saves Greece, 32; furnishes jobs, 36, 48f
Naxos, 34, 39
"New deal" in Athens, 13ff
Nobility, Roman: as governing class, 85, 91f; composition of, 86; build political machine, 87f, 90f; economic interests of, 92f; preservation of unity of, 95; achievements of, 96; coöperation with knights, 100f; hostility to Marius, 106ff
Numidia, 72

Oligarchic parties in Athenian Empire, 51ff
Olives, growing of, 17f, 28, 64
Ostracism, 42ff

Parthia, war with, 118

Party strife in Greek cities, 51ff; in Rome, 73, 108f, 116
Pericles, 48, 49
Persian invasion, 31f
Picenum, 68
Pisistratus, 27, 30
Plutarch, Life of Solon, 13; Life of Pericles, 48
Pompey, 103; as lieutenant of Sulla, 74, 109; ambition of, 109f, 112; suppresses rebellion of Sulla's opponents, 74, 109; defeats Sertorius in Spain, 74, 110; returns to help crush slave revolt, 74, 110; unites with Crassus, 74, 111; suppresses piracy, 112; conquers Mithridates, 75, 78, 112; disbands army, 79, 112; attempts to provide land for his veterans, 68, 75, 113ff; enters First Triumvirate, 75, 117; alliance with senate against Caesar, 119
Pontus, see Mithridates
Praetors, 81, 83, 84, 88, 94f
Proletariat in Italy, 67ff, 97f, 113, 115
Prosperity led to unemployment, 29, 52
Provinces, Roman: misgovernment of, 59; need garrisons, 62; governors of, 94, 104; tribute of, 63, 102; annexed by Pompey, 113
Punic wars, 61, 63, 65 note

Rabble of Rome, 89, 98, 100f, 103, 105, 107, 111f, 116, 117
Revenues of Rome, 102

Senate, Roman: furnished continuity in government, 81; composition and powers of, 81, 83; actual supremacy of, 84ff, 94; used by nobility as party caucus, 93f; later weakness of, 101; fails to provide land for armies, 105f, 108, 114; policy in Jugurthan war, 106f; Sulla's attempt

to strengthen, 109, 111; antagonism to Pompey, 110f, 114ff; loses control of government, 118
Sertorius, 110
Sicily, 63f
Slave labor, 29, 32, 36, 52, 68f
Social War in Italy, 108
Solon: reforms of, 13ff; poems of, 13f, 16f, 26; made archon, 13ff; encourages trade, 17; changes constitution, 20ff; as founder of democracy, 25f; criminal code of, 26; success of reforms, 27
Spain, 63, 74, 75, 110
Sparta, 30, 32f, 46
Sulla, 73f, 109, 111

Teutones, 72, 106, 107
Themistocles, 31f, 36, 43
Thetes given franchise, 20ff; excluded from Councils, 22f
Treasury, Roman, 68, 105, 114
Tribes, Roman: origin of, 88; voted as units, 89; urban members of rural tribes, 90, 97f
Tribunes, 81, 83, 84, 117
Tribute of provinces, 63, 102, 113f, 116
Triumvirate, First, 75, 117f, 120
Tyranny, 27f, 30f

Unemployment in Athens, 29, 47; in Rome, 98

Varro, 69
Veto power of Roman magistrates, 81, 83, 117
Volunteers in Roman army, 66f, 69f, 113

Wheat, see Grain

Xerxes, king of Persia, 32